C. Sathiya Kumar
K. Duraiswamy

Secure Self Re-Organizing of Nodes Using Closeness Technique in Cluster MANET

Anchor Academic
Publishing

Sathiya Kumar, C., Duraiswamy, K.: Secure Self Re-Organizing of Nodes Using Closeness Technique in Cluster MANET, Hamburg, Anchor Academic Publishing 2017

Buch-ISBN: 978-3-96067-185-5
PDF-eBook-ISBN: 978-3-96067-685-0
Druck/Herstellung: Anchor Academic Publishing, Hamburg, 2017

Bibliografische Information der Deutschen Nationalbibliothek:
Die Deutsche Nationalbibliothek verzeichnet diese Publikation in der Deutschen Nationalbibliografie; detaillierte bibliografische Daten sind im Internet über http://dnb.d-nb.de abrufbar.

Bibliographical Information of the German National Library:
The German National Library lists this publication in the German National Bibliography. Detailed bibliographic data can be found at: http://dnb.d-nb.de

All rights reserved. This publication may not be reproduced, stored in a retrieval system or transmitted, in any form or by any means, electronic, mechanical, photocopying, recording or otherwise, without the prior permission of the publishers.

Das Werk einschließlich aller seiner Teile ist urheberrechtlich geschützt. Jede Verwertung außerhalb der Grenzen des Urheberrechtsgesetzes ist ohne Zustimmung des Verlages unzulässig und strafbar. Dies gilt insbesondere für Vervielfältigungen, Übersetzungen, Mikroverfilmungen und die Einspeicherung und Bearbeitung in elektronischen Systemen.

Die Wiedergabe von Gebrauchsnamen, Handelsnamen, Warenbezeichnungen usw. in diesem Werk berechtigt auch ohne besondere Kennzeichnung nicht zu der Annahme, dass solche Namen im Sinne der Warenzeichen- und Markenschutz-Gesetzgebung als frei zu betrachten wären und daher von jedermann benutzt werden dürften.

Die Informationen in diesem Werk wurden mit Sorgfalt erarbeitet. Dennoch können Fehler nicht vollständig ausgeschlossen werden und die Diplomica Verlag GmbH, die Autoren oder Übersetzer übernehmen keine juristische Verantwortung oder irgendeine Haftung für evtl. verbliebene fehlerhafte Angaben und deren Folgen.

Alle Rechte vorbehalten

© Anchor Academic Publishing, Imprint der Diplomica Verlag GmbH
Hermannstal 119k, 22119 Hamburg
http://www.diplomica-verlag.de, Hamburg 2017
Printed in Germany

ABSTRACT

Mobile ad hoc network (MANET) is defined as a self-configuring infrastructureless network used for communication by wireless links with the support of mobile devices. A MANET is referred as wireless network with independent nodes moving freely with respect to each other. Due to the independent free moves of nodes, a huge amount of packet data loss occurs in transmitting the packet from source to destination. The risk of node misbehavior is extremely high. The unsecured ad hoc network environment is initiated due to the active nature of networks and node mobility. In addition, the task of key management is more complex in ad hoc network. Due to the nature of free moving characteristics, MANET faces improper node cooperation. The main reason behind ineffective node cooperation is presence of malicious or selfish nodes. Moreover, the existence of malicious unauthenticated nodes causes insecure communication. Hence, the proposed system aims in the development of proper node cooperation, malicious node detection and secure communication in MANET.

In order to enhance the node cooperation, and malicious node detection, first research work develops a Secure Key Model (SKM). The main idea behind SKM is to cluster the nodes based on reputation and ranking. Clustering of node is reorganized on its own self with the evaluation co-operative nodes. The negative reputation value in reputation table detects malicious node. Performance evaluations are carried out. SKM achieves the high performance rate of 5-9% with 7-17% of minimum computational cost compared with the ID-based Multiple secret Key Management (IMKM).

The second research work deals with node cooperation to avoid security issues like illogical node participation, with Hybrid Approach for Node Cooperation based Clustering (HANCC) in MANET. The node cooperation among the nodes in MANET is improved by forecasting the weightage of cooperativeness of each node in the network. The evaluation of node cooperation weightage detects the illogical nodes participating in the network. Performance evaluations are carried out. HANCC achieves the node cooperativeness of 20-25% compared with the Fair, efficient and secure cooperation incentive mechanism (FESCIM) and efficient clustering and cluster head rotation scheme for wireless sensor networks (ERP-SCDS).

The third research work, secures communication by the establishment of Efficient Node Cooperation and Security (ECNS) mechanism overcomes the bottleneck of selfish nodes in MANET by creating initial authentication among nodes through node cooperation. The ENCS mechanism is capable of providing high security by avoiding the misbehavior nodes. Performance evaluations are carried out and it achieves the security level of 15-25% compared with the Value iteration algorithm (VIA) and ODMR protocol using a high-throughput (ODMRP-HT).

The final research work deals with Routing Aware Packet Reserving (RAPR) framework for end-to-end throughput maintenance. This resolves the effective resource allocation. The mobile node selects the packet which travels in shortest distance. RAPR estimates the security level of the system by end-to-end routing by controlling and clogging. The performance evaluations are carried out and system uses the resources effectively and improves the end-to-end throughput by 15%.

TABLE OF CONTENTS

	ABSTRACT		i
1	**INTRODUCTION**		**1**
	1.1	BACKGROUND	1
	1.2	STATEMENT OF THE PROBLEM	3
	1.3	SECURITY IN MANET	4
		1.3.1 Attacks in MANET	6
		1.3.1.1 Vulnerabilities of MANETs	7
		1.3.1.2 Attackers	8
		1.3.1.3 Active and passive attacks	9
		1.3.1.4 Attacks at physical layer	11
		1.3.1.5 Attacks at network layer	12
		1.3.1.6 Attacks at transport layer	14
		1.3.1.7 Attacks at data link layer	15
		1.3.2 Denial of Service Attack	15
		1.3.2.1 DoS attacks on the link layer	15
		1.3.2.2 DoS attacks on the network layer	16
		1.3.3 Channel Aware Detection	17
	1.4	NODE CLUSTERING IN MANET	18
	1.5	PURPOSE OF THE STUDY	21
	1.6	ORGANIZATION OF CHAPTERS	23
2	**LITERATURE REVIEW**		**26**
	2.1	INTRODUCTION	26
	2.2	A SECURE KEY MODEL FOR EFFICIENT NODE CLUSTERING BASED ON REPUTATION AND RANKING	26

	2.3	A HYBRID APPROACH FOR NODE CO-OPERATION BASED CLUSTERING IN MANET	35
	2.4	EFFICIENT NODE COOPERATION AND SECURITY IN MANET USING CLOSENESS – A DEGREE OF SEPARATION	44
	2.5	RESEARCH GAP	52
	2.6	OBJECTIVES OF THE RESEARCH	54
	2.7	CONTRIBUTIONS OF RESEARCH	55
3	**SECURE KEY MODEL WITH REPUTATION AND RANKING SYSTEM IN MANET**		**56**
	3.1	INTRODUCTION	56
	3.2	SECURITY ISSUES IN MANET	57
		3.2.1 Reputation Based Self Re-Organized Node Clustering	60
		3.2.1.1 Reputation management	65
		3.2.1.2 Reputation broadcast	66
		3.2.1.3 Reputation detects, filter, transform and localize	66
		3.2.1.4 Resolver	67
		3.2.1.5 Route maintenance	67
	3.3	SECURE KEY MODEL ON NODE CLUSTERING USING REPUTATION AND RANKING	69
	3.4	NODE CLUSTERING BASED ON REPUTATION AND RANKING	71
	3.5	GROUP KE MANAGEMENT	74
		3.5.1 Need for Group Key Management	74
	3.6	PSEUDO CODE FOR SECURE KEY MODEL	76
	3.7	EXPERIMENTAL EVALUATION	78

3.8	RESULTS AND DISCUSSION		79
	3.8.1	Malicious Node Detection Efficiency	79
	3.8.2	Node Reputation	80
	3.8.3	Performance Rate	82
	3.8.4	Computational Cost	84
3.9	SUMMARY		86
4	**A HYBRID APPROACH FOR NODE CO-OPERATION BASED CLUSTERING IN MANET**		**87**
4.1	INTRODUCTION		87
4.2	NEED FOR NODE CO-OPERATION BASED CLUSTERING IN MANET		88
	4.2.1	Challenges of Node Cooperation in MANET	91
		4.2.1.1 Mobility management	91
		4.2.1.2 Power control and bandwidth allocation	92
		4.2.1.3 Privacy and security	93
4.3	HYBRIDIZATION OF NODE CO-OPERATION BASED CLUSTERING		95
	4.3.1	Evaluation of Weightage of Node Cooperativeness	96
	4.3.2	Process of Self-Organization and Node Clustering Based on Cooperativeness	100
		4.3.2.1 Local activity rules to attain universal characteristics	100
		4.3.2.2 Development of understandable coordination	101

		4.3.2.3	Reduction of long-lived circumstances information	101
		4.3.2.4	Protocols capable of any topology change	101
	4.3.3		Clustering Based on Weightage and Self Organization of Nodes	102
	4.3.4		Node Clustering Using HANCC	103
	4.3.5		Algorithm for HANCC	107
4.4	EXPERIMENTAL EVALUATION			109
4.5	RESULTS AND DISCUSSIONS			109
	4.5.1		Node Cooperativeness	110
	4.5.2		Clustering Energy Dissipation	112
	4.5.3		Network Lifetime	113
4.6	SUMMARY			115

5 EFFICIENT NODE COOPERATION AND SECURITY IN MANET USING CLOSENESS TECHNIQUE   **116**

5.1	INTRODUCTION		116
5.2	VULNERABILITIES OF THE MOBILE AD HOC NETWORKS		117
	5.2.1	Lack of Secure Boundaries	118
	5.2.2	Threats from Jeopardize Nodes Inside the Network	119
	5.2.3	Lack of Centralized Management Facility	120
	5.2.4	Restricted Power Supply	122
	5.2.5	Scalability	123
5.3	ACHIEVING COOPERATION AMONG NODES		126

5.4	ENHANCING SECURITY OVER MANET		128
5.5	EFFICIENT NODE COOPERATION AND SECURITY IN MANET USING CLOSENESS TECHNIQUE		129
	5.5.1	Algorithmic Flow of ENCS Mechanism	132
5.6	PERFORMANCE EVALUATION		134
5.7	RESULTS AND DISCUSSION		135
	5.7.1	Average Information Leakage	136
	5.7.2	Packet Transmission Efficiency	137
	5.7.3	Security Level	140
	5.7.4	Average Cost	141
5.8	SUMMARY		143
6	**PACKET RESERVING AND CLOGGING CONTROL VIA ROUTING AWARE PACKET RESERVING FRAMEWORK IN MANET**		**144**
6.1	INTRODUCTION		144
6.2	KEY IDEA BEHIND ROUTING AWARE PACKET RESERVING FRAMEWORK IN MANET		148
	6.2.1	Packet Reserving on Mobile Nodes	149
	6.2.2	Single RAPR Model with Multiple Packet Flows	151
6.3	OVERVIEW OF ROUTING AWARE PACKET RESERVING FRAMEWORK IN MANET		152
	6.3.1	Algorithmic Description of RAPR Framework	153
6.4	EXPERIMENTAL SETUP OF RAPR FRAMEWORK		155
6.5	PERFORMANCE OF RAPR FRAMEWORK		156

	6.6	SUMMARY	165
7		**CONCLUSION AND FUTURE WORK**	**166**
	7.1	CONCLUSIONS	166
	7.2	FUTURE WORK	168
		REFERENCES	**170**

CHAPTER 1

INTRODUCTION

1.1 BACKGROUND

A Mobile ad hoc network (MANET) is a system of wireless mobile nodes that dynamically self-organize in random and momentary network topologies. A MANET is group of wireless networks consisting of a number of mobile nodes. Nodes in MANET connect and disconnect from the network dynamically. There is no permanent set of infrastructure and centralized administration in MANET. Nodes are organized and interconnected through wireless interface. The self-motivated nature of such type networks makes it extremely vulnerable to different link attacks. The essential needs for a protected networking are secure protocols, ensuring that the privacy, accessibility, authenticity and honesty of network. Many offered security solutions for wired networks are unproductive and useless for MANET environment. As the communication takes place in an open medium, the MANET communication is more susceptible to security attacks. In the occurrence of security protocol, the effects against different attacks are reduced. Therefore, the success of MANET communication greatly depends on the relationship of the participating mobile nodes.

A MANET is described by deficient in infrastructure, lack of centralized administration, recurrent mobility of nodes, network separation and wireless links. These characters indictate that the usual wire line security solutions are not directly applicable in MANET. Certainly, the properties represent that the establishment of a public key infrastructure, is an unwieldy task in such networks.

Propagation of packet to the entire network is an essential process and includes broad applications in the MANET. The basic approach for transition is blind flooding, in which each node is compelled to retransmit the data whenever it obtains a packet for the first time. Blind flooding creates many repeated broadcasting. These repeated transmissions cause a serious trouble, referred as the transmission storm difficulty in which repeated packets leads to communication congestion and contention.

A MANET is a completely on-the-fly network utilized to maintain the idea of any time and any place transmission. MANET is an infrastructure-less network with a set of wireless mobile hosts to structure a temporary network without the support of any wired base stations. Each mobile node in such a network functions not only as a node but also as a router. The intrinsic restrictions of the MANET, such as insufficient resources and dynamic topologies, need a suitable routing protocol. The protocol design for such an environment requires straightforward, well-organized and robust structure. The methods that broadcast packets in the MANET are relatively unusual from that in the wired network, since a node transmits a packet, then all its neighbors receive that packet under the promiscuous receive mode.

Recent work on providing security comprises a fully-distributed Identification based Multiple secret Keys Management scheme (IMKM) facilitating an efficient key method. It involves an interaction of ID-based multiple secret and threshold cryptography. IMKM eliminates public key distribution using certificate authentication. In addition IMKM provides efficient key update and key revocation schemes. The nodes are clustered and needs a Cluster Heads (CHs) to participate in key construction. The updated cluster head shares the keys on establishing a threshold sharing of the master secret key. Multiple secret keys scheme is able to withstand cryptanalysis and periodically updates share keys of CHs with a predefined time interval. The scheme does not require the exchange or signing of any additional messages. At last, the method supports improved performance by reducing computation and communication overheads. Efficient group key agreement provides authentication without authenticating signatures and needs only one round.

1.2   STATEMENT OF THE PROBLEM

Ensuring secure communication in ad hoc network is extremely challenging due to dynamic nature of the ad hoc network. The difficulty in MANET communication is that the data broadcast is insecure due to lack of centralized management. MANET is a division of ad hoc network working in wireless infrastructure-less environment in the way of self-configuring communication with the mobile devices. Each node or mobile device in a MANET is independent to each other moving without self-control in any route resulting in insecure communication. The independent behavior of node flow changed the interaction link to other devices or nodes frequently. The absence of fixed infrastructure in shared wireless medium results in node mobility and limited resources of mobile devices. Due to the limited resource in communication, the bandwidth is restricted. Additionally, error-prone communication links by key management is difficult to implement in ad hoc networks.

The information is broadcast with a secure private key. Group Key Agreement (GKA) protocol is the common protocol generally used in secure transmission. GKA protocol permits two or more parties to agree on common group key and exchange information over insecure channel. GKA provides mutual key authentication among parties involved in the communication.

The limitation of GKA protocol for transmission is its overcoming nature with the establishment of Authenticated Group Key Agreement (AGKAP) protocol applications in cooperative, distributed and self organized ad hoc networks. Design of secure and well-organized protocol for group key agreement gains much concentration as an important research area. The group key management protocol is also less efficient in the transmission of packets. Major researches are needed to be handled in the key management issues for securing MANET using clusters.

1.3   SECURITY IN MANET

Wireless Mesh Networks (WMNs) are noted as a standard choice for Internet Service Providers (ISPs) in broadcasting the information over wireless access. The WMNs are estimated to integrate the characteristics of self-organization, self-healing, and self-configuration for high consistency and scalability. In addition to the numerous advantages, the WMNs require security guarantees due to its open medium, shared architecture and inconsistent topology.

A MANET is an independent set of mobile nodes which communicate over moderately bandwidth restricted wireless links. MANET varies from predictable wireless networks, such as cellular networks and IEEE 802.11, an infrastructure mode networks as self-organizing. The infrastructure networks are self-containing i.e., the nodes communicates openly with each other lacking reliance on centralized infrastructures such as base stations. Additionally, MANET is self organizing and adaptive in the way of structuring and de-structuring on-the-fly without the need for any system administration.

These exclusive characters make MANET popular for situations which will need fast network use, such as search and rescue operations. The decentralized property of MANET, specifically the deficiency of centralized entities offers a better application work nature. The avoidance of single point of disappointments makes these network models also perfect for military and commercial applications that require high level of robustness. But some challenging security issues are to be concentrated before MANET is set for extensive commercial or military deployment.

One of the major security issues in MANET is trust management. Trust is usually recognized and handled in wired and other wireless networks using centralized entities like Centralized Authority (CA) or Key Distribution Center (KDC). The lack of centralized entities in MANET creates trust management security issue as a challenging task. The inaccessibility of trusted authorities also builds crisis to achieve essential functions such as the revocation of distribution centre. Another attractive MANET security difficulty is the issue of false accusation in the existence of malicious nodes. The false accusation tries to prove the valid node as malicious node resulting in removal of legitimate node from the network. The malicious node causes several communication difficulties such as gap of opportunity problem.

In MANET, certification systems play a vital role to attain network security. Controlling the issue of certificate cancellation in wired network is simple compared to the MANET. In wired network when the certificate of a malicious node get canceled then the certificate authorities append the information about the cancelled node into the Certificate Revocation Lists (CRLs). Otherwise, they transmit the CRLs to each and every node present in the network or either saves them on an open repositories. But the certificate revocation is a difficult task in MANET and also this usual method of certificate revocation is not valuable for MANET due to lack of centralized repositories and trusted authorities. A method is required for MANET to cancel the certificate of malicious nodes after detecting the first misbehavior of nodes.

The wireless technology makes MANET more susceptible to security attacks and due to this the established security methods does not offer a novel solution to MANET. A new protocol needs to be urbanized to overcome the disadvantage in the traditional security methods such as distribution centre. Symmetric key cryptography method requires trusted third party and vital repositories to preserve information about the node whose certificate is get cancelled. But these standard security methods fail in providing the preferred security in the case of wireless networks such as MANET. In other words, the capacity of the standard security approaches is only restricted to the wired networks and to some extent in the wireless networks because the number of security problems is less in wireless networks compared to wired networks.

1.3.1 Attacks in MANET

A MANET is an infrastructure-less category network containing number of mobile nodes with wireless network boundary. In order to establish communication among nodes, the nodes enthusiastically launch paths among one another. The character and outline of such networks make it interesting to several types of attackers. The section discusses different types of attacks on various layers under protocol stack. Various types of attacker try different approaches to drop off the network performance and throughput. The main attention is on routing and security issues related with mobile ad hoc networks which are necessary in order to offer secure communication. On the basis of the character of attacks on communication, the attacks against MANET are classified into two types, namely, active and passive attacks. Also the attackers against a network are classified into two groups namely, insider and outsider. An outside attacker is not a legal user of the network but an insider attacker is a certified node and a component of the routing mechanism on MANET.

1.3.1.1 Vulnerabilities of MANETs

A MANET is vulnerable to different attacks not only from exterior but also from within the network itself. Ad hoc networks are essentially subjected to several vulnerability issues as follows:

Dynamic Topology: In MANET, nodes connect and disconnect from the network dynamically and travel independently. Due to such type character, there is no permanent set of topology mechanism in MANET. The node with insufficient physical security becomes malicious node and minimizes the network performance.

Wireless Links: As the nodes in such networks are interrelated through wireless interface that makes it extremely vulnerable to link attacks. The bandwidths of wireless networks are not as much of wired networks and offers less bandwidth. The less restricted bandwidth draws many attackers to stop normal communication among nodes.

Cooperativeness: In MANET, all routing protocols believe that nodes offer secure communication. But some nodes become malicious nodes which interrupt the network process by modifying routing information.

Lack of clear line of defense: There is no clear line of protection mechanism available in the MANET. Attacks come from any directions. Attackers attack the network either within the network or outside the network.

Limited resources: The MANET includes various collections of devices such as laptops, computers, and mobile phones and so on. All of such devices consist of different storage capacity, processing speed and computational cost. This attracts the attackers to concentrate on new attacks.

1.3.1.2 Attackers

There are various types of attackers present in MANET. They attempt to minimize the performance of network. The various attackers are categorized as shown in Figure 1.1.

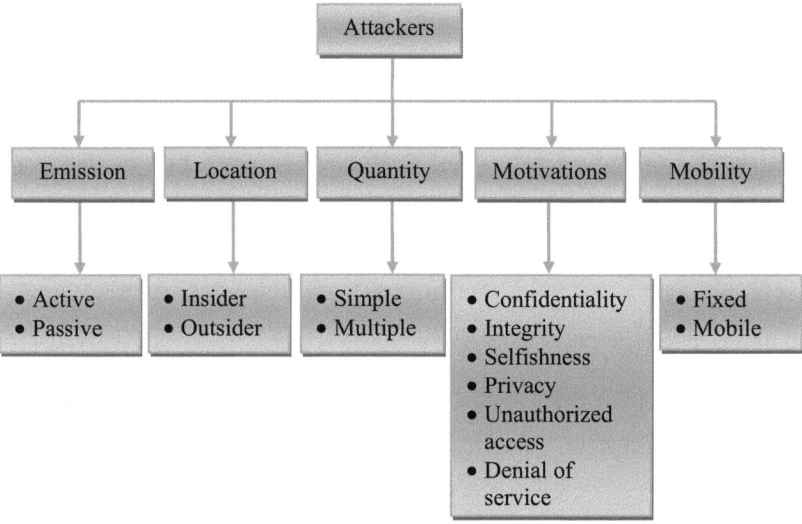

Figure 1.1 Classifications of Attackers

Figure 1.1 describes the classification of attackers in MANET into five major types in two levels. The first level of attack arises on the fundamental means of the ad hoc network such as routing like emission, location and quantity. The second level of attacks attempts to break the security methods engaged in the network such as motivations and mobility.

1.3.1.3 Active and passive attacks

A MANET is more vulnerable to passive attacks. A passive attack does not change the data transmitted within the network. But it comprises the unauthorized listening to the network traffic or gathers data from it. Passive attacker does not interrupt the process of a routing protocol but tries to find the significant data from routed traffic.

Identification of such type of attacks is complex since the process of network itself does not get affected. In order to conquer this type of attacks dominant encryption algorithms are required to encrypt the data being broadcast. The attack against the MANET is kept on increasing due to its open medium and independent nature. In addition to passive attack, another attack that plays against secure communication is active attack.

Active attacks are very harsh attacks on the network that stop message flow between the nodes. But active attacks are of inside or outside type. Active outside attacks are handled by outside basis that do not belong to the network. Inside attacks are from malicious nodes which are part of the network. Internal attacks are more rigorous and inflexible to detect than external attacks. These attacks make unauthorized access to network that supports the attacker to make changes such as alteration of packets, denial of service and congestion.

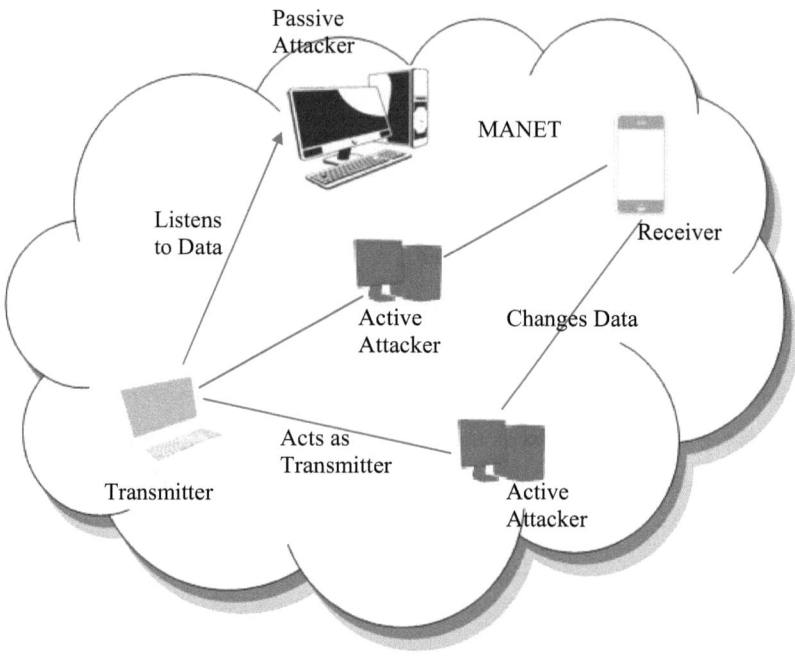

Figure 1.2 Active and Passive Attacks in MANET

Figure 1.2 describes the active and passive attacks in MANET. The passive attacker listens to the data broadcasted in the network. The active attacker acts as transmitter and changes the data transmitted to the receiver. Detecting the active attacks is more difficult compared to passive attacks. The nature of MANET formulates them vulnerable to many new attacks. The attacks in different layers of the network protocol stack are described in Table 1.1.

Table 1.1 Attacks on Protocols

Layer	Types of Attacks
Application	Malicious code, Data corruption, Viruses and Worms
Transport	Session hijacking attack and SYN flooding attack
Network	Blackhole, Wormhole, Grayhole, Link spoofing, Rushing attack, Replay attack, Sybil attack, Resource consumption attack and Link withholding attack
Data Link	Selfish Misbehavior, Malicious Behavior, Traffic Analysis
Physical	Eavesdropping, Jamming and Active interference

The attacks on physical layer are hardware related and require support from hardware origins. These attacks are straightforward to perform as compared to other attacks. They do not need the entire knowledge of technology. Some of the attacks detected at physical layer comprise eavesdropping, intrusion and congestion.

1.3.1.4 Attacks at physical layer

Eavesdropping is an interception and interpretation of messages and discussions by unintended receivers. As the transmission takes place on wireless medium, the message is easily interrupted with receiver tuned to appropriate frequency. The major intention of such attacks is to take the confidential information that is kept covered during the transmission. The information includes private key, public key, place or passwords of the nodes. Classified data is eavesdropped by tapping transmission paths, and wireless links are easier to trace.

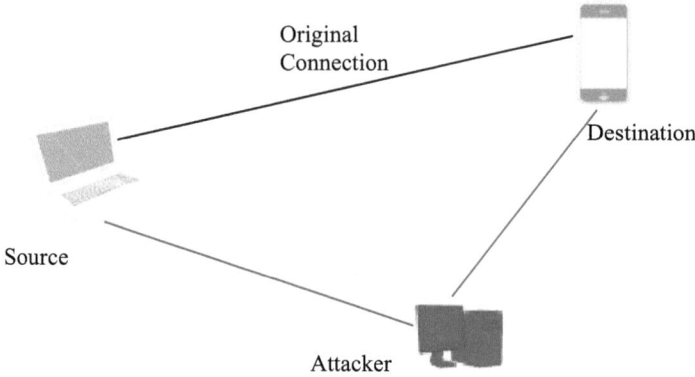

Figure 1.3 Attacks on Communication between Source and Destination

Figure 1.3 describes the attacker attacking on transmission between source and destination. Jamming is a special class of DoS attacks which are initiated by malicious node after determining the frequency of communication. An active interference is a denial of service attack which stops the wireless communication channel or alters communications. Old messages are repeated to reinitiate the data information.

1.3.1.5   Attacks at network layer

The network layer protocols allow the MANET nodes to be linked with another through hop-by-hop. In MANET, every distinct node takes choice of route to transmit the packet. So, it is very simple for malicious node to attack on such network. The essential thought behind network layer attacks is to add itself in the active path from source to destination or to take up network traffic. In such attacks, the attackers build routing loops to form harsh congestion. Various type of attacks are detected which are initiated by malicious node. Figure 1.4 describes the routing attacks by the malicious nodes.

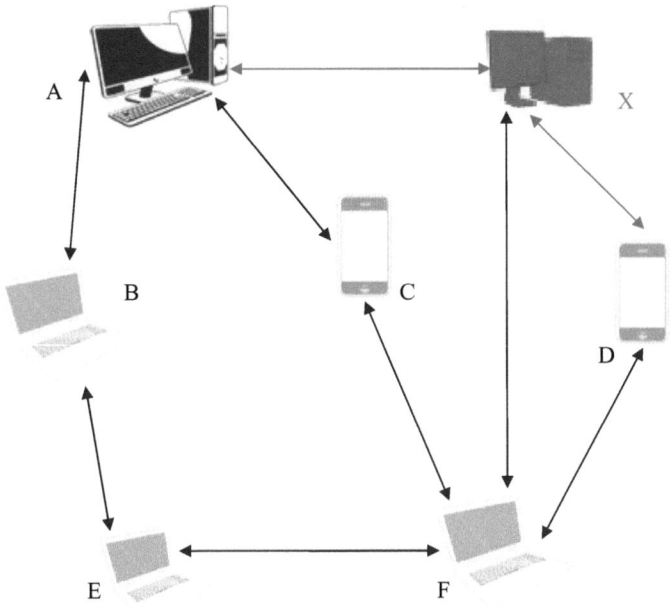

Figure 1.4   Routing Attack by Malicious Nodes

The malicious node X takes main data by locating itself between source A and destination D as shown in Figure 1.4. X also distracts the data packets swapped between A and D, resulting in significant end to end delay between A and D. The malicious node X interrupts the route path discovery process by constructing routing loops and overflow of routing tables.

In Blackhole Attack, malicious node maintains finest path to the node packet to be interrupted. On getting the request the malicious node forwards a false respond with extremely short route. In wormhole attack, malicious node obtains data packet at one location in the network and channels them to another malicious node. Rushing Attacks are essentially against the on-demand routing protocols. These types of attacks threaten the path discovery process.

1.3.1.6 Attacks at transport layer

Attacker in Session Hijacking acquires the benefit to develop the insecure session after its initial setup. In this attack, the attacker spoofs the injured party node's IP address, discovers the right sequence number i.e. estimated by the target and then initiates various DoS attacks. In Session Hijacking, the malicious node attempts to gather secure data like passwords, secret keys, logon names and other information from nodes. Session Hijacking attacks are also known as address attack and affect the transmission protocol like Transmission Control Protocol (TCP).

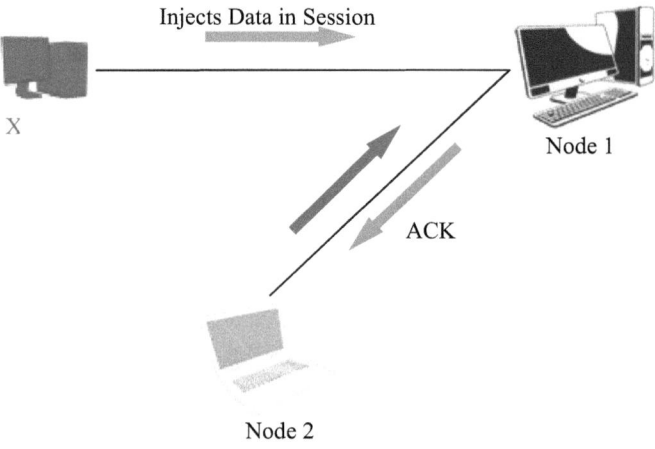

Figure 1.5 Session Hijacking

Figure 1.5 describes the Session Hijacking. The TCP- acknowledgement (ACK) tempest trouble arises when malicious node initiates a TCP session hijacking attack. The attacker X adds session data, and node 1 forwards acknowledgement packet to node 2. Packet does not hold any sequence number that node 2 is expecting. The attack is seen when node 2 receives the packet and tries to resynchronize the TCP session with node 1. This process is repeated over and over that leads to ACK tempest. Application layer protocols are also vulnerable to many DoS attacks.

1.3.1.7 Attacks at data link layer

Selfish misbehavior of node straightforwardly changes the self-performance of nodes and does not obstruct the action of the network. The main objective of malicious node is to interrupt regular operation of routing protocol. The collision of such attack is enlarged when the communication takes place between adjacent nodes.

The significant attack at data link layer is the DoS attack. These types of threats created a malicious action with the support of node co-operation that forms harsh security risks. In the presence of node cooperation, it is very complex to identify the cooperation routing. The cooperation route emerges like a usual route but guides to rigorous problems. For example, node cooperation involves in the communication but drops some packets resulting in degradation of service quality being offered by network. A detailed overview of DoS attack is described in the following section.

1.3.2 Denial of Service Attack

A DoS attack is an occurrence that reduces or removes a network's power to perform its expected function. The hardware failures, software errors, resource collapses, environmental constraints, or any complex communications between these factors cause DoS. The DoS attacks on the link layer and network layer are summarized below:

1.3.2.1 DoS attacks on the link layer

IEEE 802.11 Medium Access Control (MAC) protocol is used as the link layer protocol for MANET. IEEE 802.11 MAC is vulnerable to DoS attacks and utilizes its binary exponential back-off scheme. Because a successful broadcast results in a smaller conflict window, a constantly broadcasting node always confine the channel and causes other nodes to back off continually. A customized back-off scheme solves DoS attack by offering the back-off timer from the receiver end. Additionally, the Network Allocation Vector (NAV) field in the Request to Send/Clear to Send (RTS/CTS) frames represents another vulnerability to DoS attacks. Since a malicious node is conscious of the time interval of the current transmission in its neighborhood, it forwards few bits to interrupt the current link-layer frames with an insignificant energy cost.

1.3.2.2 DoS attacks on the network layer

DoS attacks on network layer normally categorized into three, namely, resource deficiency, routing interference and forwarding denial.

In a resource deficiency attack, malicious nodes add additional control or data packets into the network. For example, a malicious node keeps forwarding different messages to its adjacent node. Since the sequence numbers or fake target address is changed each time, an attacker's neighbors are unable to distinguish the messages as fake ones or new requests. If the malicious node forwards these fake messages at a high speed, its neighbors spends much resources, like bandwidth, CPU sequences and battery power, to face fake messages.

A typical example of this attack is Blackhole in which an attacker initiating the Blackhole Attack could direct all packets to some destination and then discard them. Another type of routing interruption attack is so called wormhole. To begin the wormhole attack, two malicious nodes N1 and N2 cooperate with each other via a private network connection, such that N1 forwards the packets received from other nodes directly to N2 through the wormhole. N2 rebroadcast the received packets to another area of the network.

1.3.3 Channel Aware Detection

The WMN is a multi-hop network which depends on mesh routers to send the packets to the destination. A successful association among routers is the basis for a trustworthy network. Cryptography solutions are utilized to defend the mesh routers from most of the routing protocol attacks like selective forwarding, Gray hole, Blackhole and Wormhole Attacks. But, if the routers are liberal, the attacker is allowed to access the public/private keys of the liberal routers and then crack through the cryptographic system. Therefore, to attain absolute security in a network, it is ideal to use cryptographic solutions as a first line of protection and non-cryptographic solutions as a second line of protection.

Most of the existing studies on selective forwarding attacks concentrate on attack detection under the statement of an error-free wireless channel. An additional realistic and demand scenario that packet falling is due to Grayhole Attacks or normal loss events such as medium access crash or worst channel quality. Specifically, a Channel Aware Detection (CAD) algorithm is developed to effectively detecting the selective forwarding attackers by sorting out the standard channel losses.

The CAD algorithm is based on two measures, namely, channel evaluation and traffic monitoring. The measure of channel evaluation is to approximate the normal loss rate due to worst channel quality or medium access crash. The measure of traffic monitoring is to monitor the definite loss rate. CAD involves four-fold contributions:

Channel evaluation is incorporated with traffic monitoring to attain channel-aware detection of Grayhole Attack. The Grayhole detection effectively detects selective forwarding misbehavior unseen in the usual loss events due to worst channel quality or medium access crash.

In CAD, upstream and downstream traffic monitoring is integrated to obtain a flexible detection method. In addition to Grayhole Attack, the CAD also identifies restricted transmit-power attack, on-off attack and dreadful opening attack.

The CAD algorithm is inefficient when multiple malicious nodes act in collision. The CAD is unable to provide useful information about the authenticated and unauthenticated nodes in the network. The more unauthenticated nodes involved in the communication, instead of authenticated node, lead to unsecure communication. Additionally, the unauthenticated nodes are not prevented to involve in the network communication.

1.4 NODE CLUSTERING IN MANET

Cluster-based routing is a solution to address node's diversity and to control the quantity of routing information that broadcasts inside the network. The purpose of clustering is to collect the network nodes into a number of coinciding clusters. Clustering makes promising ranked routing in which routes are traced between clusters instead of nodes. This increases the routes duration, thus reducing the amount of routing control overhead. In the cluster formation, the node coordinating the cluster activities is called as cluster head (CH).

For a clustered network, the network is grouped into clusters with one cluster head per cluster. Essentially, the clustered network transfers a thick network to a thin one that involves cluster heads and some gateways. The broadcast protocol uses a separation of nodes, called forward node set, to communicate a broadcast packet in a clustered network. Only a cluster head determines its forward node set to envelop other cluster heads within its neighborhood and within the exposure area. A non-cluster head node immediately communicates the broadcast packet if it is chosen as a forward node. The forward node set is determined by cluster heads. All the cluster heads in the network are connected to each other. Consequently, a broadcast packet is delivered to the total network ultimately. Cluster heads are chosen through a selection process. A cluster head straightforwardly connects to all the nodes in the cluster. Other members in the cluster are non-cluster head nodes. The clustered network is produced by the lowest-ID cluster algorithm.

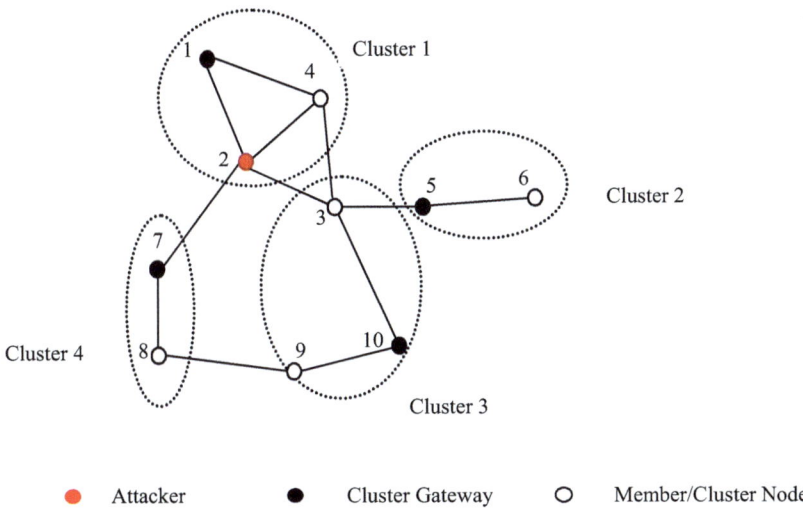

Figure 1.6 Sample Clustered Network

Figure 1.6 shows the effect of applying clustering in a network with 10 nodes. The cluster formation involves the connection of nodes into clusters groups. The node 2 acts as attacker in interrupting the communication. Other nodes are protected to deliver the packets. The pure clustered network does not sustain position of maintenance. But it will be possible to localize if a little different cluster structure strategy is applied. Once a cluster is shaped, a non-cluster head node, which are newly entered in the cluster challenges the current cluster head.

Figure 1.7 describes the cluster graph and adjacent cluster graph of the sample network as shown in Figure 1.6. If a cluster head travels into an existing cluster, the cluster head that has the higher ID will stop its role of cluster head. If a cluster head travels out of a cluster, the left non-cluster head nodes in this cluster will compute their new clusters. A node that has cluster head adjacent obtains the neighboring cluster head with the lowest ID as its new cluster head and connects in that cluster. For nodes with no cluster head adjacent, the cluster formation procedure is applied among those nodes to structure new clusters. Thus, the clusters mobility is adaptive and alters a cluster, controlled in a limited area. Thus, transmission of packet in a clustered MANET using the forward node set is able to efficiently convey the packet.

Figure 1.7 explicates the cluster graph formed in a cluster. Each cluster has its own nodes with its edges. In this the vertices refers the nodes and the edges refers the connection between the nodes. The cluster graph in Figure 1.7(a) is with good quality and dense, because all the nodes are close to each other. The cluster graph in Figure 1.7(b) is almost similar to Figure 1.7(a) with same number of nodes and edges; whereas most of the vertices are outside the cluster. The cluster graph in Figure 1.7(c) has very few connections with other nodes but lacks in internal density and hence it is not a good cluster.

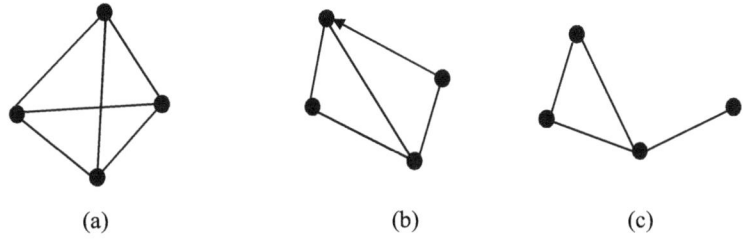

Figure 1.7 Cluster Graph and Neighbor Cluster Graph

1.5 PURPOSE OF THE STUDY

Security is the main challenge faced in protecting wireless communications especially in MANET. The security test reveals that many techniques provide strong privacy protection but wormhole attacks are difficult to prevent. These existing techniques support a secure shared key based on-demand for packet data but offers an unsecure communication.

In MANET topology, crisis occurs mainly due to the attacks that affect the network. A dynamic method is required to employ topology control algorithms in MANET to avoid topology problems. Network topology among MANET varies due to mobility and thus, it unable to maintain the network connectivity.

The cryptographic protocols concentrates on providing secure communication but also affected by diverse attacks. The attacks present in the networks and the root of that attack is also avoided. But the drawback is that the attacks on encrypted protocol are unavoidable. For the attacks like Blackhole, Grayhole, Wormhole and Rushing attack, no algorithms is launched still now and above all attack problems are still faced by MANET.

The possible solution to attacks is by performing node clustering and deriving cluster heads. Cluster heads are combined and used to avoid attacks but at the same time a key security is required to solve the attacks. The data transmission through the cluster nodes is efficient regarding energy but the congestion at the cluster heads raises. Key security along with clustering is necessary to avoid loss of packets or prevention from attacks.

A fully-distributed identification based multiple secrets key management for a secure communication using a protocol of group key management is proposed. But the disadvantages in IMKM are bandwidth usage is limited for a secure communication and consumes several rounds to recognize the secure channel. But the main drawback is that the communication between the nodes and the clustering processes are inefficient.

Misbehavior of nodes also causes problems in MANET. Routing misbehavior is also a difficult problem in providing security during transmission as the nodes drops the packets before transmitting. The packet dropping problem is avoided by using reputation based method which mainly avoid when an attacker resets a poor reputation by rejoining the system with a new identity (whitewashing attacks). The existence of delay problems keeps on increasing due to addition of nodes resulting in inefficient packet delivery to destination node in given period of time.

Nodes in the networks are scattered reducing the efficiency in communication. Cluster-based routing is a resolution to solve nodes diversity and to control the amount of routing information that propagates inside the MANET. The nodes in the network are clustered for secure ad hoc communication. A secure key model is provided for ad hoc network with efficient node clustering based on reputation and ranking model. An improvement in the reliability of the network is required to provide a fast transmission. The reputation technique is necessary to find the unauthenticated nodes involved in the communication.

In addition, the reputation and ranking models are employed to detect the misbehavior, and selfish nodes within the network communication. Determination of unauthenticated nodes is essential to avoid the adversary acts performing in MANET. The nodes co-operation is necessary to perform clustering and in recognizing cluster head. The cluster head formation helps in ranking.

A secure transmission between the source and destination plays a vital role in the MANET communication. To provide the security in communication, a key is incorporated with the information. To decide the secret keys in authenticating group, an authenticated group key agreement protocol is essential. There are several security issues generated by the selfish nodes in MANET and to improve the cooperativeness among the mobile nodes in MANET, it is necessary to ensure the node cooperation among the nodes.

1.6　ORGANIZATION OF CHAPTERS

Chapter 1 provides a brief discussion on the security of MANET with infrastructure-less network with different attacks on each layer of the network, and clustering of nodes by providing efficient node cooperation between the nodes. Additionally the performance and organization of nodes within the network is deeply discussed.

Chapter 2 reviews the previous research work on MANET security, infrastructure-less network that is relevant for the present research. In addition, reviews related to node clustering in infrastructure-less environment for secure communication, a secure key model for efficient node clustering based on reputation and ranking, a hybrid approaches for node co-operation based clustering in MANET using the closeness between the nodes are also interpreted from the research works.

Chapter 3 provides an overview of various security related issues while constructing the network. A secure key model (SKM) with reputation and ranking system is proposed as a first research work. This model dynamically evaluates the authentication of neighboring nodes and selects the trusty nodes in the cluster to support efficient transmission of data. The nodes are clustered based on the reputation table. The model provides secure successful communication between the nodes in the network without any loss of data. The design of node clustering proves the usefulness and feasibility of secure key model approach.

Chapter 4 presents a detailed description of a secure communication framework between the nodes in the network without any loss of data and the needs for node cooperation based clustering in MANET. The second research work namely hybrid approach for node cooperation based clustering (HANCC) is efficiently designed for enhancing a secure communication over MANET by improving the node cooperation among nodes by monitoring the behavior and activity of nodes along with the weightage of node cooperation. The work evaluates the performance results of the secure communication framework for hybrid approach using node cooperation based clustering.

Chapter 5 describes a mechanism to avoid the misbehavior nodes from replacing the security associations with unidentified nodes. The third research work ENCS is designed for enhancing cooperation of nodes and secures communication by adopting the closeness technique.

Chapter 6 focuses on end-to-end route awareness and represents the end-to-end route quality in terms of path lifetimes. The fourth research work Routing Aware Packet Reserving (RAPR) framework is developed in MANET that takes into account both the clogging state and the end-to-end throughput maintenance. RAPR is complimentary system to packet reserve that utilizes only local routing information. RAPR framework local routing information contains the node clustering, cooperation and high security level, which provides the maximal throughput among the contending flows. Finally, Chapter 7 provides the concluding remarks and suggestions for future work.

CHAPTER 2

LITERATURE REVIEW

2.1 INTRODUCTION

An ad hoc network is referred as wireless network and provides a wireless network communication without using infrastructure mechanism. Ad hoc is a Latin word and has the meaning "for this purpose". A mobile ad hoc network is a part of ad hoc network defined as a self-configuring infrastructure-less network, each communicated by wireless links with the help of mobile devices. The nodes in the ad hoc network are independent of each other and free to move. Since nodes are independent, packet losses are found to occur while transferring the packets from source to destination. Due to the dynamic nature of network and node mobility, the unsecure ad hoc network loses packets. Each node or device in a MANET can move freely in any direction. Always some changes occur in the communication links.

2.2 A SECURE KEY MODEL FOR EFFICIENT NODE CLUSTERING BASED ON REPUTATION AND RANKING

Privacy plays a major role in forwarding a packet. Privacy-preserve routing is vital for ad hoc networks that entail stronger privacy protection. Data packets and control packets are still linkable and distinguishable in the old schemes but they do not tender inclusive unlinkability or unobservability property. Hence, Wan et al (2012) presented capable privacy requirements concerning privacy-preserving routing in mobile ad hoc networks. An Unobservable Routing Protocol (USOR) was designed and it provided unlinkability and content unobservability to almost all forms of packets. USOR is capable, because it formed a new merging of cluster signature and ID-based encryption for route discovery. The security examination exhibits that USOR offers strong privacy protection as well as it provided security against attacks which are caused because of node compromise. But wormhole attacks were not prevented using USOR.

Thus, to provide protection against wormhole attacks a security protocol is to be proposed which is basically a difficult task. For communication anonymity, (Sankara & Bhagyaveni 2008) used Secure On demand position based private routing protocol (SO2P). It provided security in mobile ad hoc networks, by means of developing a cryptography algorithm to prevent message hacking. Global Positioning System (GPS) provided the position information of nodes for which privacy was more important. GPS obtained the position information of nodes in the network by a terminal node which behaved like a server. All the information about the terminal nodes present in ad hoc network was recorded by the server with the process of GPS system. The position information was prohibited from internal and external hackers by SO2P. It was performed using a secure routing algorithm in MANET to identify optimal path to reach the destination. Because of security mechanisms, SO2P faced some trouble in routing performance such as high packet loss ratio, less throughput, more time in end to end connection delay. Since SO2P was used under on demand basis, the secure communication might not be an efficient one.

MANET is to be secure from attacks and must be dynamic in providing security (Pankaj & Rajender 2009). Advancement in algorithms and protocols were mandatory for a secure ad hoc network because of heavy rise in security threats. Attackers or malicious nodes affect communication process and it could be avoided using Encrypted Dynamic Source Routing (EDSR). EDSR was also used to prevent numerous types of Denial-of-Service attacks. If malicious agents were found on the pathway of forwarding a packet, EDSR could drop the data packet or acknowledgment, thus preventing malicious node not to get the right information. Data packets were delivered to their destinations by EDSR but when different malicious agents were presented, it drops the packet which was to be forwarded.

Nodes might also cause problems while packets were to be received by a particular node. The nodes that were engaged in routing and forwarding must have cooperation then only the MANET performs perfectly. Steps were to be taken to make a system work properly even during the existence of malicious nodes. The performances of MANET were greatly affected because of selfish or malicious nodes. Such misbehavior nodes were to be managed. Praveen Sam et al (2008) considered two factors, namely, direct factor and distributed factor, called DUAL factor for the management.

As a development to reactive source-routing protocol, the DUAL factor protocol was designed for MANET. DUAL factor holds the components namely, the observer, the trust analyzer, the reputation scheme and the route analyzer. These components were available in every node.

In DUAL factor each node traced the character of its next-hop neighbors. If any event was found to be suspicious, data to be forwarded was given to the reputation scheme. The node activity could be based on the topology created among the network.

In MANET topology control was a challenging problem. K-edge connected topology control algorithms were designed in order to build robust topologies for mobile networks but it seemed to be insufficient. Normally in networks, node moves at diverse speeds and hence, consistently applying k values for localized topology control algorithms in any local graph was not useful. Hence, a dynamic method was presented by Nishiyama et al (2012) to use k-edge connected topology control algorithms in MANET. The proposed dynamic method automatically decided the appropriate k value for all local graphs based on local information. The trade-off among topology control and reliability was compromised by using scalable topology control algorithms. Network topology among MANET varied due to mobility and thus it could not manage the network connectivity. The above mentioned was a well known problem, but has yet to be solved. Topology problem arose mainly due to the attacks that affected the network.

The great increase in network based applications had resulted in numerous security leaks. The cryptographic protocols which provide secure communication were also affected by diverse attacks. The network traffic and host activities were monitored by Intrusion Detection Systems (IDSs) in order to avoid impacts caused by unauthorized accesses and attacks. But the traditional misuse-based and anomaly-based IDSs were vulnerable to attacks that affected the encrypted protocols because they were always concerned of payload contents inspection. An anomaly-based detection system with the help of strategically distributed Monitoring Stubs (MSs) was presented by Fadlullah et al (2010). The encrypted traffic was identified by MSs which remove features for detecting the attacks. MSs also trace back the originating network of the attack. The approach was called as DTRAB because it aimed on both Detection and TRAceBack in the monitoring stubs level. But the drawback was that attacks on encrypted protocols were not avoided.

MANET was a dynamic wireless network developed without any preceding infrastructure and so each node could behave like a router and MANET had no restriction (Khokar et al 2010). So it can be accessed by any legitimate network users and malicious attackers. The main challenge for MANET even during the existence of malicious nodes was the development of robust security solution which must secure it from routing attacks. Solutions based on cryptography and key management to avoid attackers was promising, but based on resource constraints (limited bandwidth and battery power) they led to heavy traffic loads in exchanging and confirming the keys. Tradeoffs among effectiveness and efficiency were not good as well as quite solutions provide better results in the presence of one malicious node but were not suited when multiple attackers are present. The existing security solutions of wire networks could be enforced directly to MANET but they were more vulnerable to security attacks.

MANET should be provided with security because of the usage of wireless transmission medium that was more vulnerable to attacks. In MANET, analogously diverse forms of attacks were present and an efficient way was in need to identify them. Hence, a semantic security method was designed by Mamatha & Sharma (2010): It was highly secure because it focused on detecting misbehaving links, number of packets dropped and malicious nodes correspondingly. The performance of identification and avoidance of malicious nodes, launch packet dropping and message tampering attacks. The proposed security scheme was strong and highly secure. Reactive methods could be employed instead of proactive methods because in packet forwarding, attacks were tedious problem to be prevented. Using the above mentioned technique, by increasing the node density, the effect of attacks could be tested and analyzed. The attacks like blackhole, grayhole, wormhole, rushing attack etc., were still in existence because no algorithms had been launched earlier.

A MANET had large number of communicating hosts which form network topology with wireless communication media. In Quality of Service

(QoS) based communication networks, the problem of stringent end-to-end requirement was to be clarified and for that MANET communication produced a change in communication technology. Normally, complex distributed systems faced many challenges and the main one was the routing problem which depends on a predefined set of customer preferences. It is too critical to provide assurance for quality-of-service and so the author focused on the issue. Hence, Llewellyn et al (2011) made a modification in a cluster-based QoS routing algorithm for MANET which needed to provide fault tolerance. Providing fault tolerance was a hardest one in QoS which forms a link failure-prone environment. Using Fully Distributed Cluster-Based (FDCB) routing protocol, the scalability problems in centralized routing were avoided. The fully distributed cluster-based method was identical to hierarchical routing where every cluster node kept QoS information for other cluster members. Shared global states which were unmanageable and avoided because of FDCB's distributed nature. For route discovery, initial latency was provided by FDCB's distributed routing. Cluster heads were combined and could be used to avoid attacks but without providing key security it could not be solved.

Balancing of power consumption between Cluster Heads (CHs) was processed by increasing the coverage time of a clustered wireless sensor network. A model proposed by Shu & Krunz (2010) used both intra and inter cluster traffic because clustering minimized energy consumption but increased communication burdens on CH's. The approach governed both the deterministic and stochastic models for maximizing the coverage time. In the deterministic approach, the location of the sensor and the CH was known. So a joint algorithm for connecting the sensor and CH-to-CH matrix was designed. In the stochastic model, this could not be done because the location was unknown and hence, a sensing region was assumed, where the sensors were uniformly distributed. Balancing power consumption was attained by designing two ideas namely, the routing-aware optimal cluster planning and the clustering-aware optimal random relay. Usage of different types of Medium Access Controls (MACs) (e.g., Carrier Sense Multiple Access with Collision Avoidance (CSMA/CA), Time Division Multiple Access (TDMA), hybrid Time Division Multiple Access/Code Division Multiple Access (TDMA/CDMA)) in determined algorithm was an issue. The data transmission through the cluster nodes comparatively reduced the energy than the existing systems, but it had a disadvantage that the traffic at the cluster heads increased.

Dang & Wu (2010) inspected distributed clustering method and designed Delay-Tolerant Mobile Networks (DTMNs) which was a cluster based routing protocol. Grouping mobile nodes that were having identical mobility pattern into a cluster and then, sharing resources (such as buffer space) was the idea of DTMN for overhead reduction and load balancing which aimed to attain capable and scalable routing in DTMN. In mobile nodes, communication flow was not so efficient and in nodal contact estimation, possible errors might occur, so probability, convergence and stability were main issues in distributed clustering in DTMN. The DTMN functions were identified and particular node could make decision about joining or leaving a cluster depending on contact change among the cluster.

Once clusters were formed for inter cluster communications, gateway nodes were found. Key security could be provided along with clustering to avoid loss of packets or prevention from attacks.

A key management in cluster-based MANET was a needed one and it was hard to implement. Li & Liu (2010) designed a fully-distributed ID-based multiple secrets key management scheme for a secure communication using a protocol of group key management. By combining ID-based multiple secrets and threshold cryptography the IMKM was established. Certificate-based authenticated public key distribution was not needed anymore for IMKM. For key update and key revocation methods, it provides capable mechanisms. Those mechanisms directed to be more suitable, economic, adaptable, scalable, and autonomous key management for MANET. Highly dynamic topologies and varying link qualities of ad hoc networks were addressed by generating a master secret key and it was distributed by all cluster heads. But the drawback in IMKM was that it consumes more bandwidth usage for a secure communication. The clustering with IMKM is also unreliable and it took several rounds to identify the secure channel. Yogita et al (2014), proposed improved Location aided Cluster based Routing Protocol with Key Management scheme with key distribution to generate a secure communication among nodes.

A pairwise key distribution was mandatory for wireless sensor networks because sensor nodes are susceptible to physical capture. Kwon et al (2009) proposed a location-based pairwise key pre-distribution scheme. The scheme obtained higher connectivity and flexible with less resources even during the presence of errors. Full and Random Pairwise key predistribution (FRP) used deployment knowledge and path key offering method. Key predistribution with deployment knowledge was processed first. Secondly, Shared Key Discovery (SKD) was employed. Once pairwise keys were not found by SKD, then extra key establishment was mandatory. After SKD, path key establishment with path key offering was employed. However, sensor node's constrained capabilities were the problems, because public key cryptography was tough. Achieving higher connectivity was still a great problem because large resources were accompanied and deployment errors could disturb those connectivity severely. Kun & Li (2014) proposed pairwise key management with different security level to each node in the wireless sensor networks and the compromised nodes cannot disclose the key information in the wireless networks which have higher security level.

In case of no network infrastructure self-healing key distribution schemes will be useful and the lost session keys can be recovered by group users, using self-healing mechanism. In case of unreliable network, specifically in infrastructure-less wireless network (messages may get lost) establishing group keys were also suitable. Hence, an efficient threshold self-healing key distribution method with good properties was proposed by Han et al (2009). With respect to network conditions, the lost data could be recovered by involving the distance between two broadcasts. A new user could be sponsored by the user having more threshold-value in order to combine in the group in consequences session without the knowledge of group manager. The storage overhead of the self healing key distribution at each group user was a polynomial over a finite field (no increase with the number of sessions). Forward and backward securities were not maintained by key distribution. Thus, self-healing key distribution method with original threshold was not secure.

Secure communication in ad hoc wireless networks was mandatory, because communication signals were normally available in a non secure form (openly) and so they were mostly affected by attacks. Moreover, due to the absence of central coordination and shared wireless medium they were greatly be affected by attacks compared to that of wired networks. Nodes behaved like both hosts and routers and with the help of multi-hop communication path they are interconnected. Interconnection happens mainly for forwarding and receiving packets to or from other nodes. So, Sumathy & Upendra (2010) designed a key exchange and encryption mechanism. In that, MAC address was used as an extra parameter denoted as message specific key for encryption and data was forwarded between nodes. In spanning tree fashion nodes organization was done, because formation of cycles were avoided and exchanging occurs only with neighbors which are authenticated. If the particular node was not the expected recipient, re-encryption of message neighborhood key was made and transmission would take place with its authenticated neighboring nodes. The above said process was repeated until destination node was identified but it was a time consuming process. The drawback of the technique was consuming high bandwidth for a secure key exchange. The key storage and the message storage at the node level were not employed in the proposed technique.

2.3 A HYBRID APPROACH FOR NODE CO-OPERATION BASED CLUSTERING IN MANET

Routing misbehavior in MANET was a considerable one because of its open structure. Routing protocols for MANET depend on the assumption that completely cooperative nodes could only take part. Many routing misbehaviors were present and one among them is that, some nodes might be involved in route discovery and maintenance processes but they will fail to forward data packets. The route fails to forward packets, because it may be selfish, overloaded, broken, or malicious. So, to avoid routing misbehavior Liu et al (2007) implemented the two way ACKnowledgement (2ACK) method. The main idea behind 2ACK was to receive the acknowledgements from two different hops in order to identify the misbehaving node in routing. Hence, 2ACK avoided the routing problems by detecting misbehaving node which is also referred as network-layer technique. But, route with two hops received acknowledgements in opposite direction which caused data traffic collision.

In multihop networks like mobile ad hoc networks, a node could behave rudely by dropping other packets to save battery life, because of which the whole network performance was degraded. Reputation based models have been introduced (Abbas et al 2010) to avoid node misbehavior and it was also used to avoid whitewashing attacks. Whitewashing means that if a node had poor reputation on its identity it would be changed to form a new one and would be escaped from the consequences because of its bad actions. It led the performance of reputation based models worst. Reputation based method behaves like an obstacle in whitewashing attacks. In the proposed method, every node must pay an entry fee to use network services. Selfish nodes could no longer whitewash as it needed to pay the entry fee whenever it entered the network. Watchdog mechanism was also adopted, in which reputations were performed at every node in the network. Reputation table was maintained in watchdog mechanism to note the reputation of one hop neighbors. The drawback of proposed method was that newcomers were not allowed. Blackhole attacks were also major problem creating attacks.

Mohmoud et al (2012) focused on the selfish nodes that distract proper node cooperation. A Fair, Efficient, and Secure Cooperation Incentive Mechanism termed FESCIM were developed to stimulate the node cooperation. The FESCIM mechanism performed a fair charging principle by modifying the source and destination nodes when both of them profit from the packet transmission. FESCIM employed hashing operations to make the node cooperation more effective. Hash operation in the ACK packets reduced the degree of digital-signature operations. However, FESCIM failed in the process of identifying misbehaving nodes. FESCIM droped the packets due to mobility, bad channel, maliciously and frequently dropping packets resulting in malicious behavior causing less security.

A malicious node forms a blackhole attack on MANET, which found the route from a source to a destination and modified sequence number and hop count of the routing message. Su (2011) designed intrusion detection system nodes that were employed in MANET to detect and prevent blackhole attacks. The IDS nodes are put to sniff mode to perform Anti-Blackhole

Mechanism (ABM) function. ABM was used to find a suspicious value of a node regarding to the difference among the routing messages which were routed from the node. A block message denoting to isolate the malicious node was sent to every node on the network by IDS, only if the suspicious value was more than threshold. Even, Ad hoc On-demand Distance Routing (AODV) provides a network connection when the number of IDS could not able to cover most of the area, because of less processing loads and memory consumption. To identify whether routing message was new AODV uses sequence number. Malicious node executed Blackhole AODV (BAODV) routing algorithm to avoid blackhole attacks. Normal node implemented a mildly modified AODV, called Modified AODV (MAODV), to conduct normal routing. IDS node implemented ABM to identify blackhole nodes and block message was presented. Hence, privacy was to be provided for nodes but threats based on privacy also affected the nodes.

Privacy threat was the major issue in multihop wireless networks due to the open wireless medium, in which attacks such as traffic analysis and flow tracing were initiated effortlessly by a malicious attacker. Fan et al (2011) designed a network coding based on privacy-preserving method in regards to traffic analysis, flow tracing like size correlation, time correlation and message content correlation. By trimming each message to be of the similar length, size correlation could be blocked in network coding method. Using inherent buffering method of network coding, time correlation could be resisted. Using "mixing" feature of network coding, message content correlation could be avoided. Two efficient privacy-preserving techniques were designed along with homomorphic encryption on Global Encoding Vectors (GEVs). The methods were packet flow untraceability and message content confidentiality that were proposed for preventing the traffic analysis attacks. Calculation on incoming messages was achieved by intermediate nodes which were allowed by network coding. Then, security was to be provided to avoid attacks.

During the existence of eavesdroppers, wireless networks connectivity would be diminished by information-theoretic security constraints. The security constraint motivates those networks for enhanced modeling and develops techniques which were robust to eavesdropping. Zhou et al (2011) considered the secure connections from a transmitter to the legitimate receiver(s) over fading channels, where the legitimate nodes and eavesdroppers were all randomly located. There were two forms of eavesdroppers, namely, non-colluding eavesdroppers and colluding eavesdroppers.

Multiple transmit antenna elements based nodes had a secure connectivity by the development of a directional antenna. With multi-antenna transmission techniques a large connectivity improvement was obtained. Even though security was provided, mobile users suffered a lot with authentication.

In wireless networks, roaming of mobile users, was ultimately high and authentication to be provided to mobile users was challenging. He et al (2011) designed a privacy-preserving universal authentication protocol (shortly termed as Priauth). It provided authentication against both eavesdroppers and foreign servers. Efficiency was obtained by the establishment of session key. Assumption was made as the attacker has full control against overall communication channels (among user, foreign server, home server), i.e., it might intercept, insert, delete, or modify any message running through the channel. Mainly, four forms of threats were there for user authentication namely, message en route threat, false mobile user threat, DoS attack and deposit-case attack. Here a roaming user, a foreign server and a home server were involved. In Priauth, foreign server established a session key with roaming user before it is authenticated. In Priauth, foreign servers used the Revocation List (RL) to verify that the roaming user moved from the home server was revoked or not.

Security often dealt with cost regarding performance degradation, which should be evaluated and it was in the case of Wireless Ad hoc Networks (WANETs) because it provided communications over a shared wireless channel without previous infrastructure. Zhang et al (2011) proposed a network model in which the asymptotic behaviors of secure throughput and delay were noted and when the network size was huge the probability of neighboring nodes having a fundamental security association was evaluated. A secure communication method without Secure Link Augmentation (SLA) was used and its performance was analyzed. Achievable secure network performance was estimated when SLA was allowed. Upper bounds on the secure throughput are presented with or without SLA. Throughput maintenance was also a major thing and capacity of wireless networks should be decreased.

In order to increase the capacity of wireless networks, Multi-Input Multi-Output (MIMO) method was used. Capacity scaling laws, for MIMO ad hoc networks was examined. Jiang et al (2011) identified the achievable throughput of each node by increasing the number of nodes in the network. zero-forcing beamforming (ZFBF) scheme was mainly used to exploit the profits of antenna arrays at a node. ZFBF held the two main attributes of MIMO namely; spatial multiplexing and interference cancellation. In spatial multiplexing, a transmitter could send numerous autonomous data streams to its expected receiver concurrently on a link. In interference cancellation, the transmission and reception vectors could be designed properly, so that the interference among numerous conflicting links could be removed. The development of upper bound was the key idea of ZFBF, for which joint consideration of spatial multiplexing and interference cancellation was needed. Both lower bound and upper bound had the same order and hence, asymptotic capacity for MIMO ad hoc network was tight. Delay might get increased because of the nodes and as a result, special care should be taken to avoid delay.

A TDMA based simple transmission method (Bhatnagar et al 2010) which reduced the delay problem occurred by the poor synchronization of the relaying nodes against Ricean channels. A Pair-wise Error Probability (PEP) was also proposed based on precoder for unsynchronized cooperative networks against Ricean (fading) channels which were uncorrelated. If transmissions were scheduled correctly, then significant coding of optimized precoder could be gained. Full diversity could also be obtained based on approximate delay profile. The drawback of the above mentioned method was that higher SNR among the relays due to wrong relaying.

Rossi et al (2011) took into account the wireless cooperative multihop networks, in which the message decoded by a node at the previous hop to cooperate in the transmission towards the next hop (with distributed space-time coding). The aim of the author was to find optimal cooperator selection approach for arbitrary topologies with links troubled by path loss and multipath fading. Through an appropriate Markov chain, the network behavior was modeled and cooperator selection process was devised as a Stochastic Shortest Path problem (SSP). A new pruning technique was developed to diminish the complexity of SSP. The technique started from the original problem and a diminished Markov chain was retrieved which was at last installed into a solver with the help of Focused Real Time Dynamic Programming (FRTDP).

The ability of mobile infostation network could be increased through short-range communications among mobile nodes and fixed infostations. Cooperation among mobile nodes was not fundamentally casual for commercial applications. Yuen et al (2009) decided to present a means to generate cooperation in the contention distribution context among the selfish mobile infostation networks. Every node had an interest in all files, was the first assumption. A bilateral file exchange occurs only when the nodes obtained something which was wanted from the exchange. Capacity depends on mobility, the number of files to be declared, and node density. Downloading time of each node would decrease when nodes had implicit cooperation. Energy cost for transmitting one file was balanced. Analysis had proven that the networking performance of the file exchange method was based on node mobility and density. As number of files in the network increases, the fairness and throughput of the network also got improved. If nodes had overlapping interest, then network performance was highly corrupted. Cooperation enforcement should be addressable and should not increase to an extent.

Every user had its own rights in autonomous MANET but the cooperation enforcement performance problems were the major concern. The problems had to be resolved to perform network functioning, like packet forwarding which causes trouble under noise and imperfect monitoring. So, Ji et al (2006) focused on cooperation enforcement in autonomous MANET which causes noise and imperfect observation. The fundamental packet-forwarding function was considered by means of game models with information which were not correct. Belief-based packet forwarding framework was used to enforce cooperation to reduce noise and imperfect observation. Nodes were needed to figure out the future actions of other nodes which depend on their own imperfect observations. The inference process held noise and imperfect observations and to compute them traffic monitoring approaches were considered. It was carried out by each node which keeps track of its neighbors' actions. Encryption techniques could be taken into account to provide security in routing.

An encryption technique designed by Sumathy & Upendra (2010) was used as a safe key alternate over the nodes in the network. The positive side of the security scheme was that encryption was done twice using two diverse encryption schemes (neighborhood key and message specific key). Hence more security was provided. Two forms of secrecy were also employed and they were backward and forward secrecy. In the backward secrecy, a network's novel member was not able to access the data that was transferred before the member joined the group. In the forward secrecy, a member was not able to access the data that was transferred after the member goes away from the group. Normally, the topology changes by adding or removing a member, at that time a novel neighborhood key was generated and given to all authenticated neighbors. The neighborhood key for each authenticated neighbor was applicable when group communication was to be carried out in a secure manner. The neighbor detection method was to identity-free and was preceded with handshake procedure among several pair of neighbors. For key exchanges, handshaking procedure was followed among the given node and its newly identified neighbors. Key management based protection could be employed for secure communication.

Li & Liu (2010) proposed a system for a secure communication using group key management protocol. It used ID supported confirmation key over ad hoc network for safe forwarding. Key management was used in cluster-based MANET, because of the dynamic nature of the network and offering a secure communication is challenging. The master secret key was developed for addressing the dynamic topologies and link qualities. The key was distributed by all cluster-heads. As a result, not only attack and failure were avoided but it led to flexible key update methods. The number of rounds and bandwidth usage were also minimized by a significant one round ID-based Authenticated Group Key Agreement (ID-AGKA) protocol. All primary security concerns are also satisfied by ID-AGKA. Even though, the

ID-AGKA provided efficient packet delivery ratio through clustering operations, the time taken for transmission was bit high.

Most of the node cooperation was performed using the concepts of clustering. One such proposed method by Ashok Kumar et al (2011) was Energy Efficient Clustering and Cluster Head Rotation Scheme (ERP-SCDS) for WSN. ERP-SCDS supported clustering formation but it was time consuming and clustering energy dissipation was low. In addition ERP-SCDS faced the difficulty of large overhead in external information forwarding for cluster maintenance. Also Dong et al (2011) developed ODMRP protocol using a High-Throughput metric. Although ODMRP-HT was capable of providing high throughput and the efficiency in improving security in terms of quality was still lower.

Node distribution was not uniform in wireless networks; hence energy consumption by nodes was more in cluster-based sensor networks. Yu et al (2012) designed a cluster-based routing protocol for WSN along with nonuniform node distribution. The protocol involved an Energy-Aware Clustering Algorithm (EACA) and a cluster-based routing algorithm. Clusters of even sizes were generated based on competition range which was used by EACA. In the covered area, the forwarding tasks of the nodes was improved by routing algorithms, which was done by choosing nodes with higher energy by cluster heads. Then, next hop of cluster heads were fewer member nodes and obtains load balance among cluster heads. Cluster heads with higher energy was chosen based on the ratio of average residual energy of neighbor nodes and the residual energy of the node itself.

2.4 EFFICIENT NODE COOPERATION AND SECURITY IN MANET USING CLOSENESS – A DEGREE OF SEPARATION

A Sensor network consists of many sensor nodes and those networks were normally found to be in mesh structure. Mostly, nodes in sensor networks were static and some sensor nodes behaved like a router which forward messages from one neighborhood to another. In node connectivity, changes result due to the disruptions like transmission power changes, or loss of synchronization within neighboring nodes in wireless communication. Node connectivity was more important in providing security because, attacks may also spoil network connectivity. Sensors were conscious about their immediate neighbors, but still it should constantly manage its view, so a mechanism called continuous neighbor discovery was proposed by Cohen & Kapchits (2011). Two nodes were denoted as neighboring nodes only when they have straight wireless connectivity and it must be always bidirectional. Sensors in networks with heavy traffic do not need to initiate any particular neighbor discovery protocol instead of which the node could identify its neighbor by listening to the channel and could reform the lost connectivity.

Technologies for connectivity maintenance and message exchange between decentralized nodes were to be designed, so wireless multi-hop network adopted wireless communication technologies. Wireless resource allocation needed centralized coordinator as it is in heavy lack and so the design of medium a ccess control protocols was difficult for throughput enhancement in the wireless ad hoc networks. The receiver blocking problem, was the major one in MAC protocol design and resulted in reduced of throughput performance. Feng et al (2013) used Multiple Receiver Transmission (MRT) and Fast Network allocation vector Truncation (FNT) mechanisms to solve the receiver blocking problem (no involvement of extra control channels). The throughput performance was still to be enhanced and so the Adaptive Receiver Transmission (ART) along with dynamic adjustment of pointed receiver was presented. Effectiveness of ART protocol was validated by deriving analytical model.

Bu et al (2011) combined continuous user authentication and intrusion detection in the design of Value Iteration Algorithm (VIA) to provide high security to MANET. However, the value iteration-based solution for measuring the Gittins Index process only operated for a MANET with a small number of nodes and a small number of states as well as observation states. For a large network with a variety of nodes, the value iteration based solution become computationally intractable and was inefficient in providing security to nodes.

Message delivery in MANET was difficult because there was no connectivity in the network. Hence, a better idea was to find a route which provides good data delivery and produces low delay in a disconnected network. Daly & Haahr (2009) proposed social network analysis metrics that was in use for significant message delivery (forwarding solution) in broken network. The metrics depended on social analysis of node's past interactions and consisted of three locally calculated factors, namely, a node's "betweenness" centrality (with the help of ego networks), a node's social "similarity" to the destination node and a node's secure energy association with the destination node.

Among the three metrics that were evaluated separately, average utility resulted in better overall delivery performance but congestion was caused due to highly central nodes. Congestion had to be avoided and it could be done only by transferring other node's data.

In many applications of MANET, mobile nodes shared and used data of alternative mobile nodes. In such type of application, avoiding the degradation of data availability during network partitioning was really a challenging problem. Specifically, in MANET because of free mobility of nodes, connectivity problem happened frequently and makes data in different networks to be unreachable to each other. Hara (2010) target was to quantify the consequences of mobility on data availability from various points of view. Rather than considering particular applications or data replication or diffusion protocols, many common metrics could be assumed to quantify data availability. For data replication protocols, the factors affecting the performance were number of data items to be replicated on connected mobile nodes and time taken and quantity of changes for group of connected mobile nodes.

For data diffusion protocols, factors for performance were the capability (fast) of data items to be allocated to a large number of mobile nodes. Mobility of nodes caused performance degradation in MANET.

The mobile nodes, mobility and resource restrictions resulted in network partitioning or performance reduction in MANET. Network partition was resulted often due to the free movement of nodes and thus, leads to data inaccessibility for some nodes, which was a vital performance metric. Replication of data at nodes was development to enhance data accessibility to carry on with periodic network partitioning. Replication normally enhanced data accessibility and minimizes query delay. Maximization of data accessibility could be done by restricting a node not to hold same replica that was held by other nodes which increased own query delay. Choi et al (2012) and Shoba & Neha (2014) denoted the problem of selfishness regarding replica allocation in MANET, i.e., a selfish node never divided its own memory space to hold replica and the problem was termed as selfish replica allocation. Selfish node identification and new replica allocation approaches were used to hold the selfish replica allocation. Some selfish nodes were there which includes false data while data was to be transmitted.

In wireless sensor networks, sensor nodes added false data at the time of data aggregation and data forwarding. Ozdemir & Çam (2010) designed a Data Aggregation and Authentication protocol (DAA), to incorporate false data detection with data aggregation and confidentiality. Data aggregation was formed in accordance with false data detection, the observing nodes of each data aggregator performed data aggregation and corresponding small amount message authentication codes were computed for verification of data at their pairmates. Confidential data transmission was carried out as data integrity was authenticated in the encrypted data by the sensor nodes of two continuous data aggregators. One of the candidate aggregators among the two dropped its application and ran the secure Data Aggregator Selection Protocol (DASP) again. The procedure got continued till minimum intermediate nodes among any two consecutive data aggregator were present. Each sensor node should be capable of both aggregating and forwarding of data to advance network security and efficiency. Data forwarding had one major problem i.e., there was a delay in the transmission of packets.

Mobility of relay nodes was improved by delay-tolerant ad hoc networks to make permanent connectivity. Thus facilitate communication among nodes, which were out of range of each other. Delivery delay was to be minimized, so that the data to be delivered was replicated in the network. Altman et al (2008) designed an analytical method that allowed quantifying tradeoffs within resources and performance measures (energy and delay). The coding effect on performance of the network while accessing parameters, which were governed by routing, was also studied. Tradeoff between energy and probability, which gave a successful delivery during the presence of limited storage capacity at a node were examined. In order to overcome disconnections in Delay-Tolerant Networks (DTN), coding schemes was used in which existence of phase transitions were present. Particularly, message should be applicable for a finite amount of time (i.e., after certain deadline message is of no use). The file to be transferred was splitted into k smaller units. Splitting of file was done when the file was large enough in accordance with buffering capabilities of nodes. Those k smaller units are to be forwarded without the involvement of others. If all k frames were received at the destination, then only the message would be considered to be received in good way.

Due to propagation of packets, node mobility got decreased and power outages got increased because of disconnection in networks that occur in delay tolerant networks. Krifa et al (2008) designed store-carry and forward protocols for above mentioned problem, in which a node stored a message in its own buffer and carried it for a long duration. Capable buffer management methods were required to make decision on which messages was to be discarded. Basics of encounter-based message dissemination were also used in optimal buffer management policy which depended on global knowledge of network. Buffer management policy could be set either to decrease the average delivery delay or to increase the average delivery rate. Finally, distributed algorithm came in existence which tried to estimate the global knowledge that was needed by optimal algorithm.

Devices like Personal Digital Assistance (PDA), cell-phones with wireless interfaces form MANET and communication happened through intermediate nodes. A store and forward network architecture named as delay tolerant network had been created for challenging network environments like network connectivity damage. Chuah & Yang (2009) proposed DTN method, so the popular nodes got the coded packets by which greater message delivery ratio was got. Mitigation method had been designed to overcome data dropping attacks. For producing more coded packets, mitigation method used dynamic redundancy factor. A selfish or malicious node provides false information in control or data planes of a network coding (wireless network). If selfish nodes were launched in the control plane, attack would affect the selection of routing and in case of data plane, coded packets were corrupted by the attacker hence reconstruction of message by receiver was not possible. Selective dropping attacks based on the delivery performance of network coding were determined by the usage of Community Based (CB) model and Random Waypoint Model (RWP).

Yang et al (2012) denoted the issue in delivering data packets in mobile ad hoc networks based on reliability and time. Position-based Opportunistic Routing (POR) protocol was designed, in which forwarding nodes cache the packet that were to be received based on MAC interception. Some neighbor nodes which identified the transmission of a data packet will pose as forwarding candidates. Those candidates tried to forward the packet only, when it was sent by a best forwarder within mentioned time period. The additional latency utilized by local route recovery was diminished to an extent and the duplicate relaying was also decreased. For communication hole, a Virtual Destination-based Void Handling (VDVH) method was processed. Using VDVH the profits of greedy forwarding (e.g., large progress per hop) and opportunistic routing could be obtained when handling communication voids. Delay-Tolerant was an everlasting problem in MANET and had no end.

In delay tolerant mobile ad hoc networks, direct connectivity was no more needed and messages were delivered to their destination because of mobility of node subset which carried copies of the message. Altman & De (2011) designed a fluid approximations for class of monotone relay methods (delay tolerant ad hoc networks). The class used epidemic and two-hops routing protocols. The relay policies were upgraded with probabilistic forwarding feature in which a message was forwarded to a relay with some probability. An optimal control problem was composed where a tradeoff between delay and energy consumption was found and optimized.

In DTN, connectivity between mobile nodes was not assured even though many solutions were in existence. DTN's constant assumption was that the nodes always forwarded messages but the main problem arose when they were affected by attacks. Dini & Duca (2012) designed a reputation-based protocol for conflicting blackhole attacks. In every node, table's node forwarding reputation and for forwarding the next node, it chose the node which has highest reputation. Three basic methods were involved in the protocol namely; node lists, aging (for efficient communication) and supports changing operating conditions (of DTN) to avoid attacks. Reputation-based approach was applied to Context Aware Routing (CAR) protocol (probability-based routing protocol) to protect the messages from blackhole attack. Lower the reputation, higher the chance of node being blackhole. Dropping of packets was major problem in MANET in order to save energy.

In multihop networks like MANET, to save battery life a node dropped other packets, due to which whole network got collapsed. Reputation based models had been introduced (Abbas et al 2010) to avoid node misbehavior and whitewashing attacks. Preventing the consequences which would be caused by bad actions when a node has poor reputation and fresh one was to be started. It led the performance of reputation based models worst. Reputation based method behaved like a deterrent for whitewashing attacks. In reputation based method paying entry fee by every node was a compulsory one in order to use network services. But a selfish node could not whitewash for a long time because it needed to pay entry fee whenever it entered the network. Watchdog mechanism was also adopted, in which reputations were performed at every node in the network. Reputation table was used to note the reputation of one hop neighbors. The drawback of the method was that newcomers were not allowed. Hence, every user should had own authority than having it commonly.

In self-organized MANET, every user had their own rights which behave cooperatively like unconditionally forwarding packets for each other was not acceptable. Ji et al (2006) aimed in cooperation enforcement of self-organized mobile ad hoc networks which were with noise and imperfect observation. The basic packet-forwarding function with the help of repeated game models with no clear information was also studied. A belief-based packet forwarding framework was designed to gain cooperation-enforcement strategies which relayed on each node's past actions. Applying repeated game model was to evaluate the nodes interactions. The drawback was that two nodes were needed for carrying a packet and forwarding a packet which led to delay in delivery. Simple solution was to provide key based security in delivering a packet with node clustering concept.

A key management in cluster-based MANET was important thing. Li & Liu (2010) designed a fully-distributed IMKM for a secure communication using a protocol of group key management. Combining ID-based multiple secrets and threshold cryptography, IMKM was established. Sharing secret key among cluster heads was done using the protocol and it was distributed to its master secret key. As a result, not only attack and failure were avoided by the protocol but it also led to flexible key update methods. Number of rounds and bandwidth usage were also minimized by a significant one round ID-based authenticated group key agreement protocol. All primary security concerns are also satisfied by ID-AGKA. But the drawbacks in IMKM were that it consumes more bandwidth usage for a secure communication. The clustering with IMKM was also unreliable and it took several rounds to identify the secure channel and the communication between the nodes and clustering processes both were effectively reliable ones to communicate.

Security was the bottleneck for wireless applications because they were vulnerable to attacks. Guan et al (2012) was interested on authentication and topology control issues and developed a Joint Authentication and Topology Control (JATC) method in order to improve the throughput. JATC was an optimization problem, which needed the channel estimation rather than prior perfect channel status. With study to an authentication protocol, JATC method was designed. It improved the parameters of up-layer authentication protocol and PHY-layer transmission settings to raise resource utilization and throughput capacity of the network. JATC handled the imperfect channel knowledge and the changing topology, for that a discrete stochastic approximation approach was involved by JATC. Thus, more efficient security was to be provided with key model along with clustering concept in an advanced manner.

2.5   RESEARCH GAP

In wireless communications especially in MANET, security was the main challenge that needed to be concentrated. The security examination exhibits that USOR provided strong privacy protection between the nodes but wormhole attacks were not able to be prevented. A Secure on demand position based private routing protocol is an another security providing protocol, used for providing a shared secured key on demand for data packet but did not provide a secure communication between nodes. So it was difficult to provide security to the transmission of data without providing a secure communication between nodes.

In MANET, providing a secure communication was difficult due to the topology crisis and the attacks that affect MANET. A dynamic method was designed to employ topology control algorithms in MANET to avoid topology problems but the topology among the MANET varied due to the mobility of nodes, thus maintaining the network connectivity and node cooperation was difficult task.

There were many cryptographic protocols proposed to provide secure communication in MANET but were also affected by diverse attacks. Hence, DTRAB was established for Detection and TRAceBack in the monitoring stubs level. But it failed to avoid attacks like blackhole, grayhole, wormhole, rushing attack over an encrypted protocols. These attacks could be avoided by clustering nodes in MANET with the help of cluster heads. The Cluster heads were combined to avoid attacks but without providing key security they could not be solved. The data transmission through the cluster nodes was efficient regarding energy but the traffic at the cluster heads increased. A key security management could be provided along with clustering to avoid loss of packets or prevention from attacks.

A fully-distributed ID-based multiple secrets key management for group key management was proposed for a secure communication. But the drawbacks in IMKM were bandwidth usage for a secure communication, clustering and took several rounds to identify the secure channel. Due to this, the communication between the nodes and the clustering processes were main problem in group key management.

In a secure communication, the misbehavior of nodes might also cause problems in MANET. The routing misbehavior was avoided by implementing the 2ACK method but when misbehaving nodes participate in the route discovery, it degraded the performance in terms of dropping the packets and consumes more power.

The packet dropping problem was avoided by using reputation based method which mainly avoid whitewashing attacks. But if any new node participates in the route discovery process then there would be a delay, because they are not part of the clustered nodes. Then delay might get increased because the new node also taken into account i.e., due to delay, packets were not delivered to destination node in given period of time.

2.6   OBJECTIVES OF THE RESEARCH

The main objectives of this research work are as follows,

- To design a secure key model by clustering the nodes with group key management to provide security to the participating nodes in terms of packet transmission and routing, that helps the nodes to communicate without any loss of data and to evaluate the authentication of neighboring nodes with the help of cluster heads.
- To provide secure communication between the nodes in the MANET without any loss of data, the secure key model need the cooperation based clustering for monitoring the activity and behavior of nodes.
- To avoid the misbehavior of nodes in the clustered MANET, it is necessary to design enhanced mechanism that monitors the neighboring nodes who are participate in the communication in the cluster.
- To minimize the delay in the route discovery due to misbehavior of node, need to focus an end to end route awareness and end to end route quality in terms of path lifetimes.

2.7 CONTRIBUTIONS OF RESEARCH

The first work describes, a secure communication between nodes in MANET without data loss, using secure key model (SKM) for efficient node clustering based on reputation and ranking system. By using this model, nodes are clustered and each node maintains its own reputation table. The details are illustrated in the chapter 3.

Second research work, proposed is Hybrid Approach for Node Cooperation based Clustering (HANCC). The proposed method avoids security issues like illogical node participation to balance the cooperation among the nodes. The details are illustrated in the chapter 4.

Third work describes an Efficient Node Cooperation and Security (ENCS) mechanism. It reduces the packet loss due to security attacks using closeness technique. The mechanism for closeness technique based on reputation is illustrated in the chapter 5.

The final work, manages resource allocation with Routing Aware Packet Reserving (RAPR) framework for end-to-end throughput maintenance. It describes the approach to resolve the effective resource allocation based on node clustering, node cooperation and higher security level.

CHAPTER 3

SECURE KEY MODEL WITH REPUTATION AND RANKING SYSTEM IN MANET

3.1 INTRODUCTION

An ad hoc network is referred as wireless network with independent nodes moving freely. Due to the independent free moves, a great extent of packet data loss arises in transferring the packet from source to destination. The possibility of node misbehavior is high. The unsecure ad hoc network environment is originated due to the energetic character of networks and node mobility. In addition, the task of key management is complicated in ad hoc network.

Several researchers proposed techniques using clusters for a well-organized communication from one network to other network. The existing work offered a fully-distributed IMKM scheme for a secure communication. The group key management is handled using cryptography and ID based secret key. IMKM provides authentication to the nodes in the networks efficiently. But the drawback is that it consumes more bandwidth usage for a secure communication and the clustering with IMKM is also unreliable. Additionally, IMKM takes several rounds to identify the secure channel.

The work on self reorganizing node clusters facilitates secure ad hoc communication. The proposed work presents a Secure Key Model (SKM) for ad hoc network with efficient node clustering based on reputation and ranking model. Misbehavior and selfish nodes in ad hoc network are detected efficiently with reputation ranking. Clustering of node is reorganized on its own self with the evaluation of normal co-operative nodes. The node clustering forbids unauthorized node to involve in the communication between the nodes in ad hoc network. The simulation of secure key model is done for varying topology, node size, attack type and intensity with different pause time settings. The performance metrics used in the evaluation are node reputation count, malicious node detection efficiency, performance rate in node clustering and computation cost.

3.2　SECURITY ISSUES IN MANET

Wireless networks provide connection flexibility between users in different places. In addition, the network can be extended to any place or building without the need for a wired connection. Wireless networks are differentiated into two classification namely infrastructure networks and ad hoc networks. An Access Point (AP) acts as an essential coordinator for all nodes in infrastructure networks. The nodes are linked to the network with the support of access point. In addition, AP systematizes the connection between the Basic Set Services (BSSs), facilitating easy access of route at the time of requirement. But the limitation of handling infrastructure network is the huge volume of the routing table. Additionally, the AP is connected to the router through wire in infrastructure environment leading to unsecure communication.

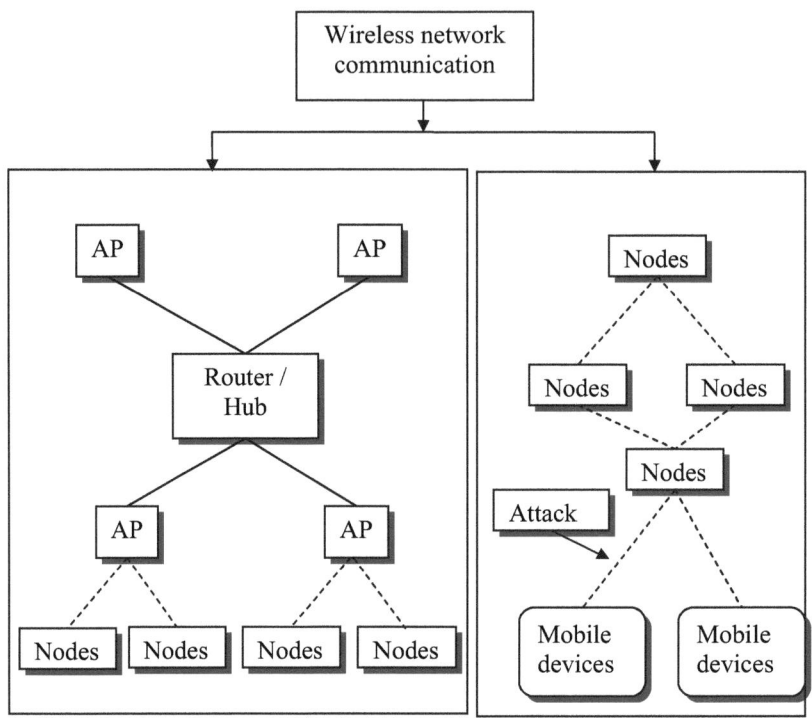

Figure 3.1 Types of Wireless Network

Figure 3.1 describes the types of wireless network communication. The dotted line represents wireless connection and the solid lines represent wired connection. The two different types of wireless communications are wired AP connection with wireless nodes and complete wireless node connection. The purpose of AP is to coordinate the nodes for better communication and to support transmission as AP is connected to router/hub. On the other hand, the complete wireless node connections are connected to mobile devices. Moreover, the possibility of attack is high on communication between mobile device and nodes. Additional concentration is required in complete wireless node connections.

Unlike in infrastructure network a central coordination point is needless in ad hoc network. Moreover, sending and receiving packets are denser than infrastructure networks. Currently, with the enormous development in wireless network applications like PDAs and cell phones, handheld computers, researchers are optimistic to progress the network services and routine. One of the demanding proposal issues in wireless ad hoc network is supporting secure mobility in MANET. The independent behavior of nodes in MANET enhances the difficulty of the routing protocols and the amount of connection flexibility. But, the possibility of permitting nodes to connect, depart, and transfer data to the network cause security challenges.

In a wireless network, a transmission range of node usually uncovers the entire network, so end-to-end communication requires routing information through some nodes. As a result, ad hoc networks are referred to as multi-hop networks. The hop is a direct link between two nodes. In an ad hoc network, nodes are termed as routers or terminals. As ad hoc network is an environment without infrastructure, the co-operation among the routers is worst. Independent nature of nodes creates the problem of routing framework leading to nodes misbehavior in the network. The misbehaved node types are referred to as selfish nodes. The lifespan of the network automatically decrease when the selfish nodes in the network increases. The main solution to address these problems is providing secure routing.

Fadlullah et al (2010) proposed techniques for securing routing in ad hoc network such as Certificate-Based Cryptography (CBC) and ID-Based Cryptography (IBC). For a fixed network, a secure communication is effectively done through Public Key Infrastructure (PKI) or a centralized certification authority. But these methods are not feasible for ad hoc network. Distribution of a signing key and Centralized Authority (CA) functionality over multiple nodes is a promising solution to this problem. In ad hoc network, the reputation mechanism is presented to dynamically evaluate the authentication of neighboring nodes. The reputation system selects the trusty nodes to support trustworthy behavior in transferring packets.

The three main goals of reputation system are providing useful information about the authenticated and unauthenticated nodes in the network, encouraging the authenticated node to involve in the communication facilitating a secure channel and discouraging the unauthenticated node. After eliminating unauthenticated node, the authenticated nodes are involved in the network communication. The ranking model is also used in ad hoc network for a secure communication. The process involved in ranking model is to rank the node based on their activities and forwarding time. Based on rank, the ranking model selects the nodes to transfer the packet data.

3.2.1 Reputation Based Self Re-Organized Node Clustering

The reputation of the node defined based on the quality of the node behaviors. The reputation systems helps the clustered nodes to collect, distribute and aggregate the information about all the nodes in the cluster based on its past behavior. Each node maintains a reputation table which contains information regarding the node's current transmission. The information maintained in reputation table is collected either directly or indirectly from each node in a MANET. The direct way to collect the reputation information of node in the network is through observation of node characteristics and the indirect way to collect the reputation information of node in the network is through observation of related other nodes characteristics with respect to specific node.

In addition to utilizing past observations in gathering reputation information, SKM presents a new reputation system. The working of reputation system in SKM facilitates the process of identifying the unauthenticated nodes. SKM uses reputation detection to ensure that old reputations fade away providing more possibility for nodes to retrieve their reputation. The authenticated node is decided based on constant behavior of the nodes in a cooperative manner.

A secondary response supports to react against any neighbor nodes with originally bad unauthenticated reputation. The wild unauthenticated nodes show early signs of node misbehavior afterwards to avoid selfish nodes from network. The response of misbehaved nodes is recorded in the reputation table in form of reputation value of nodes. The reputation value of misbehaved nodes in the network is indicated as negative. The reputation noise detection in avoiding misbehaved node and cancellation, variation test and secondary response implemented in SKM in order to increase the accuracy and reliability of the reputation system.

The reputation system in the SKM is performed with the identification of malicious nodes based on high reputation and high symmetric. The level symmetric is considered in the task of performing high symmetric rate. In SKM, Level symmetric is used in order to choose the good number of significant authenticated nodes to support in the role of selecting other nodes in the cluster. The selected other nodes based on level symmetric builds trust into other less popular nodes in the network and act as public leaders. Nodes with higher symmetry contain higher chance of getting in contact with many authenticated nodes than nodes with low symmetric.

The source of indirect reputation information is the recognition of both high symmetric and high reputation. The identification of reputation in the nodes grows even more significant in high mobility MANET network communication. As nodes are independent to each other, with few links, there is much possibility of frequent connection change causing more asymmetric nature. Argument of secure key model is nodes with higher symmetric and higher reputation are major nodes to give highly trusted authentication opinions about other nodes in MANET in a self reorganized manner. A symmetric of personality networks is used for each node to attain localized view of its adjacent nodes to permit fast reputation union and consequently higher throughput. Node clustering is performed with the reputation system and level symmetric. Node clustering based on reputation symmetric is explained below in Figure 3.2.

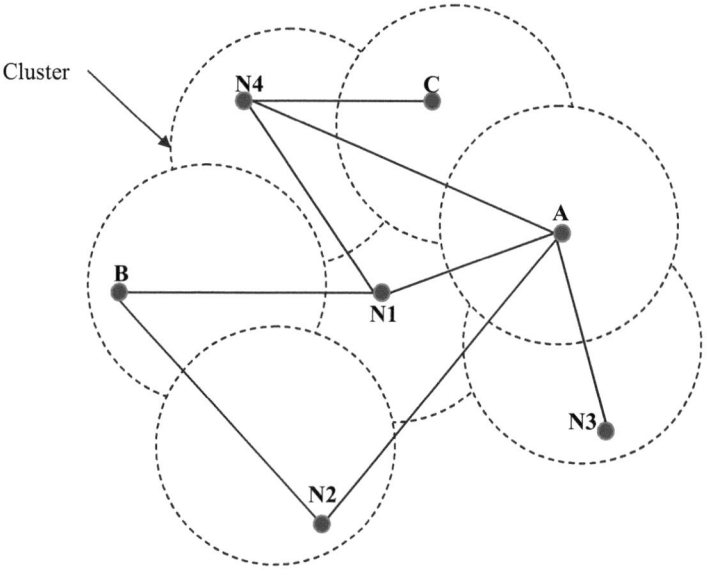

N1, N2, N3, N4 – Neighbor Nodes

Figure 3.2 Reputation Symmetric Based Node Clustering

Figure 3.2 is an example for clustered node, where N1, N2, N3, N4 are the neighbor nodes to A, B and C. In the cluster, the nodes A, B, C cannot communicate with each other without the help of its neighbor nodes. Node A possibly sends message from nodes N1 to N4 either directly or indirectly through N1-B-N2-A-N4. In indirect communication, initially node B is responsible for transferring message from N1 to N4 with the help of reputation observation of node A. As node B starts the communication, it is more important for successful message delivery. Therefore, level reputation-based symmetric approach is performed on node B. On performing level reputation-based symmetric approach, node B collects symmetric measure based on Node A's adjacent nodes reputation estimation of that node A. Indicating that node B is susceptible against attacks, as it knows the characteristics of other nodes around it through clustering. The information around node B protects it from the attacks, restricting the vulnerable ones. Hence, the implementation of level reputation-based symmetric approach makes Node B more robust against attacks.

Nodes reputation information is gathered with the aid of symmetric node characteristics. Node reputation information is classified into high, medium, uncertain, low and negative. Similarly, symmetric characteristic of nodes is categorized into high, medium and low.

Table 3.1 Reputation Table to Self Re-Organize Node Selections

		Reputation				
		High	Medium	Uncertain	Low	Negative
Symmetric	High	N4			C	N1
	Medium			A	N3	
	Low		B			N2

■ Sector 1   ■ Sector 2   ■ Sector 3   ■ Sector 4   ■ Sector 5   ■ Sector 6

Table 3.1 shows classification of experimental nodes into sectors based on their reputation and symmetric. On monitoring the state of the node regarding the characteristics like path travelled, status of node behavior and trust, the nodes are sectored to high, medium and low. As per in Table 3.1, high reputation and high symmetric in sector 1 denotes high trust. Node N4 falling into Sector 1 i.e., high reputation and high symmetric which denotes that this node holds the high trust and clear path travelled characteristics. Hence, node N4 is highly trusted with wider view of the network. Moreover, the node N4 under the high trusted sector is highly advantaged. The nodes classified as belonging to high trusted sector is exceptional from the variation test and decision-making termination time. The variation test finds the unauthenticated node and authenticated node based on low and high reputation respectively. The high reputation or authenticate node reduces termination time records.

On the other hand, nodes falling into Sector 6 are classified as misbehaving nodes due to low reputation and low symmetric which indicate the trustless characteristics. Therefore, a node N2 falls into low reputation and low symmetric which is termed as unauthenticated node as well as misbehaving node. Therefore, the presence of node with negative reputation value like node N2 is eliminated from network communication to avoid attacks. Similarly, the identified misbehavior nodes are rejected from involving in network communication.

Based on the node behavior characteristics, the nodes are categorized in reputation table as depicted in Table 3.1. Node N4 is recognized as authenticated node in Sector 1 for transferring packets by establishing trusted connection. At the same time nodes N2 is identified as unauthenticated node because the node lies in Sector 6 with untrusting connection. So, the node A rejects the connection to node N2 and searches trusted node like N4 for packet forwarding. The packet is forwarded from Node A to Node B on estimating the shortest path. So, the packet forwarding establishes connection through node N1 as it is already identified as authenticated node.

Nodes falling in sector between 1 and 4 encompass special levels of recognition and the different constraints are used to reveal their present sector. Nodes arrangement varies over time. The alteration of nodes leads to change over from high reputation to low reputation node. The higher reputation node begins to behave maliciously causing less trusted node falling to less favorable sector 6. The secure key model allows the network to develop into a multiple clusters of various trustworthiness levels. These different levels of trustworthiness tolerate higher layer applications to edge their communication only to one selected sector versus any other sectors.

Reputation procedure with a reputation table shows the interaction between the key components of reputation model. Reputation system is designed in order to offer automatic and autonomous routing decisions to the fundamental routing protocol based on the available adjacent reputations. The routing protocol used in secure key model is authenticated group key agreement protocol.

3.2.1.1 Reputation management

The major task of reputation management is the responsibility of maintaining nodes reputation records. The reputation management works in the process of managing nodes storage and retrieval with respect to nodes adjacent reputation information. Reputation management organizes the process of the other components and act as the attention point for all the events held inside the reputation system. Adjacent Reputation Record is the object that represents reputation observation. Each node holds N adjacent reputation records where N is determined by the node's memory capacity, CPU powers maintenance in updating records and other resource utilization. Nodes with higher reputation and symmetric range sufficient reputation records about other nodes in order to provide enough reporting of the nodes in its own sector. Nodes reprocess the records using termination time to provide stability in different overheads with the requirement to attain adequate reputation.

3.2.1.2 Reputation broadcast

Reputation broadcast is the process of getting oblique (indirect) reputation form. Reputation broadcast performs a selective variation test to guarantee the agreement of observation with the receiving node point of observation. Traditional variation test needs each node to judge against received oblique (indirect) reputation with its own straight reputation for a given adjacent. Any oblique (indirect) reputation is discarded with the low variation determined by a certain threshold value of nodes. The selective variation test involves the receiving node to compute the reputation of its adjacent node. Receiving node initially validates the reputation of the oblique reputation information node. If the reputation of receiving node contains higher threshold value then Node B will be trusted without additional tests. Reputation broadcast provides fast reputation union. Simultaneously, Node A asymmetric nature decreases with respect to Node B as a result of trusted node.

3.2.1.3 Reputation detects, filter, transform and localize

The computation of the straight (direct) reputations is implemented in reputation system. The reputation system calculates an overall dependency in reputation value. The reputation value at each node for all nodes determines the reputation using straight (direct) and oblique (indirect) reputation information. Each node analyzes the symmetric of reputation information in order to reveal on each adjacent reputation. The rank of assurance in the adjacent node reported oblique (indirect) reputation.

3.2.1.4 Resolver

Resolver is the responsibility of actual calculation in determining adjacent final reputation. The final reputation calculation is finalized by integrating straight (direct) and oblique (indirect) reputation avoiding reputation noise cancellation. The possibility of packet dropping by nodes is higher due to other network criteria like network jamming, intrusion. Depending on the node individual information about the average quality reported by the node's physical layer, the node is capable to correct the threshold of acceptable silent error level from that adjacent node. If the node identifies a packet loss from its adjacent node below threshold value, then node will consider the loss as noise and ignores the lost packets.

3.2.1.5 Route maintenance

The route maintenance is utilized at the time of resolver execution in detecting lower threshold value of certain adjacent node reputation. The route maintenance metric is responsible for disconnecting all the routes crossing adjacent nodes. The route maintenance process initiates a new substitute route search as required. The secure key model implementation with reputation sets the path to a special mode. The establishment of route in the network connection enabled possible transmission in the network. The special route model is capable of queuing packets emerging out on the route. The moving out packets on the path provides a queuing packet till a substitute route is determined. If the substitute route is unrecognized, then all packets queued will be dropped and a route error message will be passed to the adjacent nodes. Different components of secure key model depends on a number of observed parameters that change exact adjacent or node extensive parameters in a absolute state-machine for each node as shown in Figure 3.3.

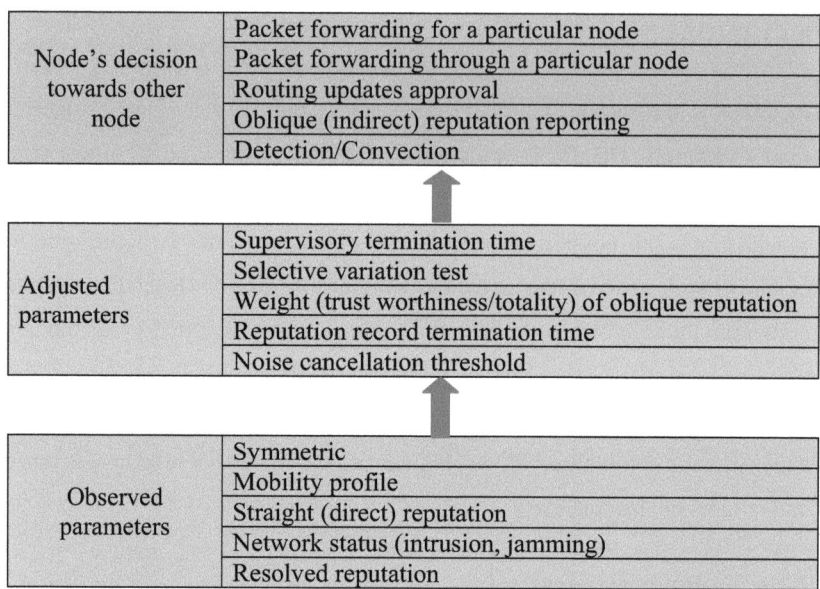

Figure 3.3 Reputation System Parameters in Reputation Table

Figure 3.3 describes the reputation parameters involved in the reputation table. The trust of nodes decision towards other node around is determined based on the adjusted parameter and observed parameter. The adjusted parameter holds metrics like supervisory termination time, selective variation test, weight (trust worthiness/totality) of oblique (indirect) reputation, reputation record termination time, noise cancellation threshold. Supervisory termination time is the time taken to terminate on reaching a decision of authenticated or unauthenticated node, selective variation test to identify unauthenticated node, reputation record termination time forecasts delivery time and noise cancellation threshold denotes identification of misbehavior node at right time. Observed parameters are symmetric for node trust verification based on symmetric values in reputation table, mobility profile for present region of mobile device, straight reputation for direct identification of node character, network Status (intrusion, jamming) and resolved reputation with status restrictions.

The reputation framework depends on symmetric and mobility as two input parameters to force the reputation system to an additional secure state in highly mobile, light and disconnected environments. The symmetric reputation based system presents integration of level symmetric and reputation. The reputation systems in secure key model propose a number of optimizations for more efficient node monitoring and trust resolution in determining authentication of the node.

3.3 SECURE KEY MODEL ON NODE CLUSTERING USING REPUTATION AND RANKING

Wireless network is always affected by attackers due to its easy access through wireless connectivity. Ad hoc network is a wireless communication struggling to provide secure network. The secure ad hoc network in an effective communication is attained with clustering process based on reputation and ranking. The clustering of nodes is defined as the formation of groups with nodes. The clustering process facilitates the recognition of cluster head from a group formation. The clustering head is identified basically with reputation values. But secure key model identifies the cluster head based on the rank decided from reputation value. The goal of reputation system is to allow nodes to construct knowledgeable choices. The choice is regarding nodes accessibility with some decisions. The decision made on the node's property support a node or prohibits it from network.

The misbehavior of the node is identified with the decision choice by the reputation system. The identification of nodes misbehavior is possible as long as the node is under observation. The elimination of misbehavior nodes from the network enhances the secure communication. In addition, the key with authenticated group key management protocol is used with reputation system improving communication as a secure one. The secure key model based on reputation and ranking for secure communication is shown in Figure 3.4.

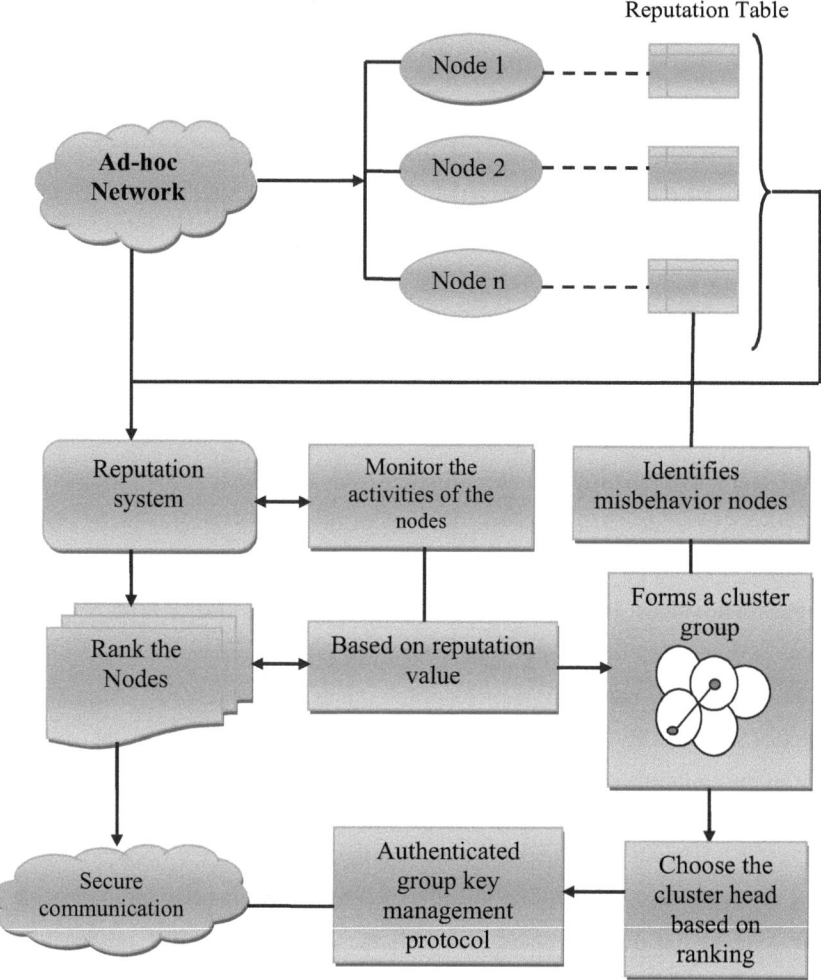

Figure 3.4 Secure Key Model Based on Reputation and Ranking

Figure 3.4 describes the secure key model based on reputation and ranking. Initially the nodes in the ad hoc network are monitored. The reason for monitoring the nodes is to form reputation table for each node. The reputation table is formulated based on the reputation parameters like Packet forwarding for a particular node, Packet forwarding through a particular node, routing updates acceptance, indirect reputation reporting and node detection/ convection. The reputation table formation leads to the reputation system process. The reputation system procedure is to monitor the nodes behavior in turn identifying the misbehaved node from the network. The elimination of misbehaved nodes is the result of reputation system. Next process involves ranking. The reputation system generates reputation value at the time of monitoring nodes. Based on the reputation value a clustering is formed with nodes. Cluster heads are decided from the group of nodes based on rank. Finally the authenticated group key agreement protocol is utilized to provide secure communication.

3.4 NODE CLUSTERING BASED ON REPUTATION AND RANKING

An ad hoc network consists of set of nodes for wireless communication. The nodes are independent of other communicating node in a wireless network environment. The nodes in the network are monitored by reputation system and are given some reputation value. Each node in the network maintains reputation table with reputation value of neighboring nodes in the network.

Node A in Figure 3.5, passes the packet data to node B only after checking out the reputation value. The reputation value of nodes decides the behavior. If a reputation value is positive, then the node is a well-behaved node. Otherwise, the node is termed as misbehaved node. For instance, if node B is identified as misbehaved node, then Node A drops the connection with it and checks out for another trusted node. Likewise, node A forms one or more secure channel to pass the data packet. Finally, the destination selects the shortest path passing the message.

Packet forwarding for a particular node
Packet forwarding through a particular node
Routing updates acceptance
Oblique reputation reporting
Detection/Convection

↓ Reputation parameter

Reputation Table	
Nodes	**Reputation Value**
N1	Negative
N2	Negative
N3	Positive
N4	Positive

↓

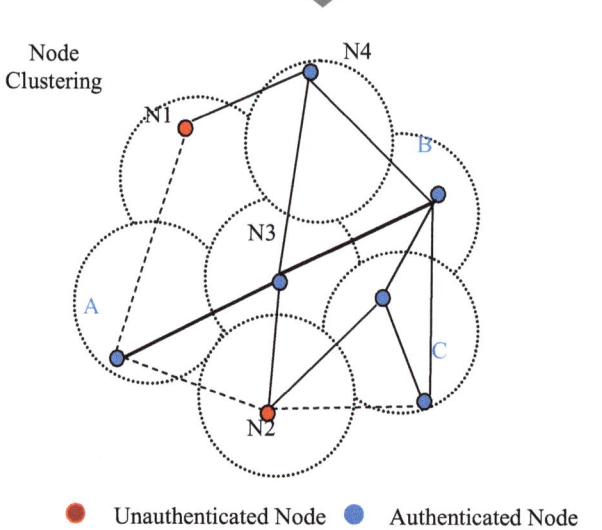

● Unauthenticated Node   ● Authenticated Node

Figure 3.5   Node Clustering Based on Reputation Value

Figure 3.5 describes the node clustering operation in detail based on the reputation value. The reputation value is generated in the reputation table with the support of level based symmetric reputation. The reputation system works determining reputation table as seen in table 3.1, for each node located into sectors with respect to evaluation metrics. The reputation table includes the reputation value for node A interconnecting node N1, N2, N3 and N4 respectively. As depicted in Table 3.1, the node N4 is detected to be authenticated with high reputation and symmetric value. On the other hand, node N1 and N2 is identified as unauthenticated node due to low reputation value in reputation table. Therefore, in Figure 3.5, node N1 and N2 is indicated in red color while authenticated nodes are indicated in blue color for node clustering based on reputation value.

The packet forwarding involves transmission from node A to node B. The node A initially determines the N1 connection but drops the packet forwarding as identifying it a misbehaved node with respect to reputation negative value falling in sector 6 of the reputation table. Node A permits N3 intermediate node for packet forwarding after recognizing it as well behaved node. Similarly the other nodes are determined. Later node B decides the shortest path for packet forwarding and allows transmission. The shortest path is decided as A $\rightarrow$ N3 $\rightarrow$ B and packet reaches destination node B in a secure way. After the process of reputation system the task of secure key model is to determine the ranking procedure.

Based on the behavior of node and cluster head, the process of ranking is done. Eventually, CH of the node is decided based on the reputation value derived from reputation table. As the clustering operation is basically performed with the integration of reputation system and level symmetric approach, it favors the election of CH. By this way of CH selection and node behavior, the ranking of node is aligned. The ranked node is aligned as a small subnet of the network. The route maintenance in MANET is handled with establishment of group key management protocol to provide secure communication.

3.5 GROUP KEY MANAGEMENT

The packet forwarding involves several secure transmissions. The major section is reputation and ranking for determining nodes behavior. In addition, the key management is involved in better communication. The group key management of the network communication normally involves several secure routing protocols scheme used by Li & Liu (2010) and Bhorkar et al (2012).

3.5.1 Need For Group Key Management

Group key management is a challenging task for key management in MANET, due to the nodes mobility and change in topology. The group key management protocols allows two or more nodes in the cluster MANET allows to exchange information among the nodes over an insecure channel using a common group key and this mutual key authentication among the nodes allows an authenticated group key management for a secure Cluster MANET. The secure key model provides an efficient Authenticated Group Key Agreement Protocol (AGKAP) for secure communication. AGKAP is implemented for cluster-based MANET as follows:

Step 1. Each cluster head $CH_i (1 \le i \le n)$ randomly chooses a key value L_i, where $L_i \in Z_q^*$.

Step 2. Each CH_i constructs a Lagrange interpolating polynomial with degree $n - 1$, as follows,

$$B_i(x) = \sum_{u=1}^{n} L_i \prod_{j=1, j \ne u}^{n} \frac{(x - K_{i,j})}{K_{i,u} - K_{i,j}} \pmod{n}$$

$$= a_{i_{n-1}} x^{n-1} + \ldots + a_{i_1} x + a_{i,0} \pmod{q} \qquad (3.1)$$

where $K_{i,j}$ is the pair-wise session key of CH_i and $CH_j (1 \le j \le n, j \ne i)$.

Step 3. Each CH_i then transmits the message $(a_{i0}, a_{i1}, ..., a_{i_n-1})$.

Step 4. After receiving the $(a_{i0}, a_{i1}, ..., a_{i_n-1})$ from other CH's, each $CH_j (1 \leq j \leq n, j \neq i)$ uses the session key $K_{j,\ i}$ to recover keys L_i, substitute $x = K_{j,i}$ in Equation (3.1),

$$B(K_{j,i}) = \left[a_{i_{n-1}} K_{j,i}^{n-1} + ... + a_{i_1} K_{j,i} + a_{i,0} \right] (\mod q) = L_i \qquad (3.2)$$

Step 5. After recovering all the keys, each CH computes the group key as follows,

$$SK = SK_j = (L_1 + L_2 + ... + L_n) P_m \qquad (3.3)$$

Step 6. After sharing the key by the group, they stated that the other group is authenticated one to share the packet data with all the others nodes.

The cluster head randomly chooses the ephemeral key for each node in the network. Each cluster head builds a Lagrange interpolating polynomial with degree less than the last node. B indicates the Lagrange interpolating polynomial and is determined with the ephemeral key values of cluster head. Each cluster head then transmits the message. After receiving the message from other cluster heads each node in the cluster uses the session key to recover ephemeral key. Each cluster head computes the group key on recovering the entire ephemeral key. The ephemeral key is assigned to each group. The ephemeral key decides the authentication of the group for communication. The group decides the trusted secure communication to other group based on the ephemeral key authentication for sharing packets. Finally, the group key management supports a secure communication in the MANET.

3.6 PSEUDO CODE FOR SECURE KEY MODEL

The pseudo code for secure key model is illustrated with the input value as nodes from $N_1, N_2,...N_n$. A detailed explanation on pseudo code for secure key model is elaborated below:

Input: **Let the nodes be $N_1, N_2,...,N_n$**
Let t, RT be threshold value, reputation table respectively.
Step 1. Compute threshold value for each node $t(N_1), t(N_2),..., t(N_n)$
Step 2. After computing $t(N_n)$,
Step 3. For each node N_i
Step 4. Form a reputation table RT_i
Step 5. Assign each reputation table RT_i to each node N_i
Step 6. End for
Step 7. Identify the best threshold value $t(N_i)$
Step 8. For each pass of packet data,
Step 9. Check the reputation table RT_i for each node Ni based on threshold value $t(N_i)$
Step 10. Form a secure channel
Step 11. For each node N_i
Step 12. Assign a rank $R(N_i)$ based on $RT(N_i)$
Step 13. Group the Nodes N_i based on threshold value $t(N_i)$ and rank R
Step 14. Choose the cluster head CH_i
Step 15. End for
Step 16. End for
Step 17. Assign a secret key for each group as detailed in AGKAP
Step 18. End
Output: Secure communication channel

The above pseudo code illustrates a secure communication channel for a secure key model. For each node in the cluster formation, reputation table is assigned individually and the best node threshold value for each node is determined. For example, consider nodes forming clustering as depicted in Figure 3.5, transmitting packet from node A to node B. As per the reputation value as well as symmetric value in reputation table (Table 3.1), node N4 is determined to be authenticated one and node N2 is misbehaving node. Therefore, form a secure channel with node N4 discarding node N2. Assign, a rank to node B based on reputation table. Then group the nodes based on threshold value and ranking, followed by selection of CH. At last, a secret key is assigned to each group, for providing secure communication.

The threshold value for each node in the reputation table is measured respectively. After computing the threshold value for all nodes, reputation Table 3.1 is constructed with reputation value. The reputation value like negative or positive is determined for each node. The best threshold value is identified for a secure channel transmission. To pass the data packets in a secure way, each node's reputation value based on the threshold value is checked.

The validation on each node identifies the misbehaved node and negotiates the node for transmitting packets. The node identifies the shortest path for delivering packets with secure channel. For each node rank is assigned and the node is grouped depending on the threshold value of nodes. The cluster head is selected from the group formation with for loop. A secret key is allocated for each group in enhancing secure communication. The secret key is assigned to each group using AGKAP. Finally, the secure communication is provided in secure key model based on reputation and ranking.

3.7 EXPERIMENTAL EVALUATION

The performance of the secure key model is estimated with simulation running on a Linux machine, with a P4-3.4GHz processor and 1GB of memory. The secure key model is implemented in NS-2 environment. The simulation area is 900x900 m^2, in which nodes move from a random starting point to a random destination, with speed of 4, 8, 12 m/s and a pause time of 3 seconds. The parameters involved in better performance of secure key models are malicious node detection efficiency, node reputation, performance rate, computational cost and bandwidth.

The computational cost of the secure key model for an efficient node clustering is low compared to IMKM model for cluster based MANET. The advantage of secure key model for an efficient node clustering based on reputation and ranking model is it consumes less time and computational costs. With greater key lengths, the advantages of secure key model for an efficient node clustering based on reputation and ranking model over IMKM increase significantly. To maintain the same security level, the work employed a greater length of key. Another advantage is that it consumes less bandwidth, less storage requirements and computational overhead. The secure key model for an efficient node clustering does not use any certificate for an authenticated group key exchange.

The scalability of the secure key model for an efficient node clustering is improved using cluster based approach depending upon reputation and ranking model to deal with the size of the subgroup in the ad hoc network. SKM minimizes the network traffic and improves the lifespan of the network. The group key distribution among the network is also good compared to an existing IMKM model for cluster based MANET.

3.8 RESULTS AND DISCUSSION

The secure key model enhances MANET communication with reputation and ranking. In addition, the authenticated group key agreement protocol is utilized to enhance the communication on validating ephemeral key with respect to node. The secure key model result is compared with existing IMKM model proposed by Li & Liu (2010) in MANET for a secure communication.

3.8.1 Malicious Node Detection Efficiency

The effective communication in secure ad hoc network is attained with clustering process based on reputation and ranking. The objective of reputation system is to permit nodes to build informed choices. The choice is about nodes accessibility with certain specific decisions. The decision made on the nodes property support a node or prohibits it from network. The malicious node is recognized with the decision choice by the reputation system. The identification of malicious node is possible as long as the node is under observation. The elimination of malicious nodes from the network enhances the secure communication.

Figure 3.6 describes the malicious node detection efficiency with respect to number of nodes. The secure key model is compared with an existing fully-distributed ID-based multiple secrets key management scheme. Based on the simulation results, the percentage of malicious node detection efficiency is forecast with different cluster formations of nodes.

Table 3.2 Malicious Node Detection Efficiency

Number of Nodes	Malicious Node Detection Efficiency (%)	
	IMKM	SKM
20	45	50
40	50	59
60	56	65
80	62	72
100	68	77
120	74	81
140	79	88
160	85	90
180	88	97

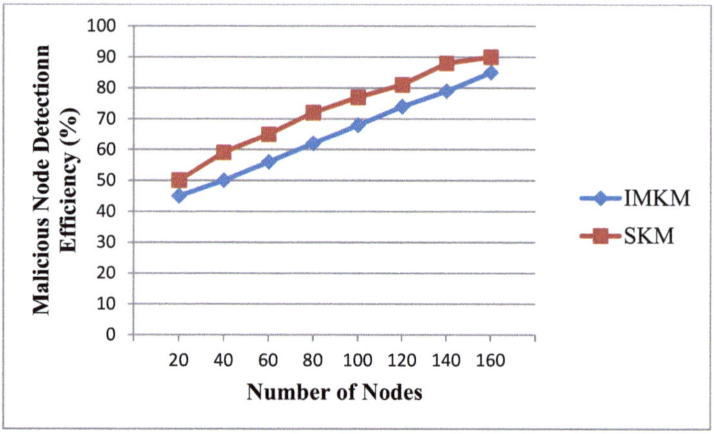

Figure 3.6 Malicious Node Detection Efficiency

3.8.2 Node Reputation

The node reputation is defined from the functioning of nodes in its symmetric characteristics. The nodes reputation is classified as high, medium or low symmetric. The reputation of the node is divided into high, medium, uncertain, low and negative with respect to the high, medium and low symmetric as shown Table 3.1. The node reputation represents the characteristics of the nodes like state, path travelled and trust. The reputation value for each node is determined with the threshold value in the reputation table for each node separately. After computing the threshold value for all nodes, reputation table is built with reputation value and symmetric value. The reputation value like negative or positive is determined for each node from the reputation table. The best threshold value is identified for a secure channel transmission.

Table 3.3 Node Reputation

No. of Node	Node Reputation (%)	
	IMKM	SKM
20	40	46
40	47	55
60	52	59
80	60	65
100	63	69
120	66	73
140	72	79
160	78	81
180	80	87

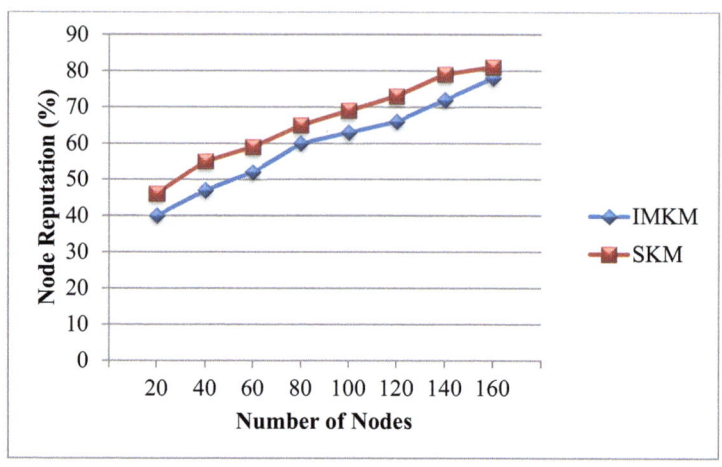

Figure 3.7 Node Reputation

Figure 3.7 describes node reputation with respect to maximum number of nodes. To pass the data packets in a secure way each nodes reputation value based on the threshold value is checked. The validation on each node identifies the misbehaved node and negotiates the node for transmitting packets. The node identifies the shortest path for delivering packets with secure channel. SKM is compared with an existing fully-distributed ID-based multiple secrets key management scheme.

3.8.3 Performance Rate

The performance rate of the node clustering is measured to prove the better performance of secure key model. The construction of node cluster is based on the reputation value derived from the reputation table. In addition, the clustering procedure engages the node cluster based on both behavior and reputation value of the nodes. The clustering process results with formation of group involving nodes. The cluster heads is selected based on rank. The performance rate of node clustering is determined for both secure key model and IMKM.

Table 3.4 Clustered Nodes vs. Performance Rate

Clustered Nodes	Performance Rate (kb)	
	IMKM	SKM
20	2112	2234
40	2136	2258
60	2146	2267
80	2155	2279
100	2231	2348
120	2247	2389
140	2254	2405
160	2268	2481
180	2375	2589

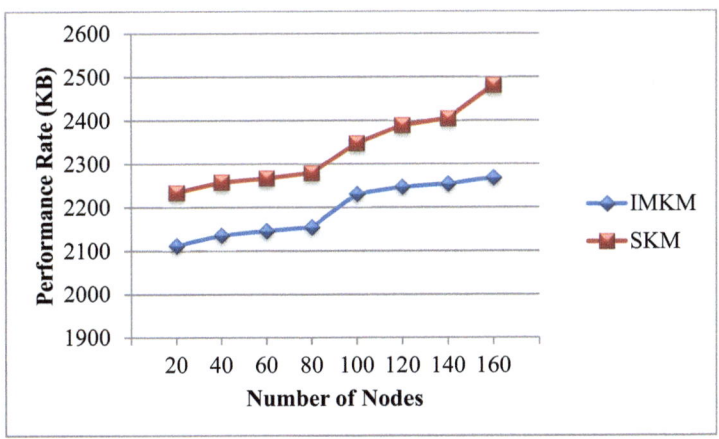

Figure 3.8 Clustered Nodes vs. Performance Rate

3.8.4 Computational Cost

Computational cost indicates the processing speed and time of clustering nodes, reputation system, group key generation and ranking. Computation cost denotes the time taken to reputation system in negotiating malicious node from network, ranking nodes. In addition, time taken in clustering nodes determining cluster head and grouping key management with authentication. Figure 3.9 exhibits the time behavior of SKM and existing IMKM with respect to the computational cost.

Table 3.5 Computational Cost

Number of Nodes	Computational Cost (Seconds)	
	IMKM	SKM
20	2.16	1.87
40	2.55	2.23
60	4.46	3.73
80	4.23	3.55
100	6.41	5.26
120	7.49	6.40
140	8.66	7.59
160	8.92	7.84
180	9.08	7.99

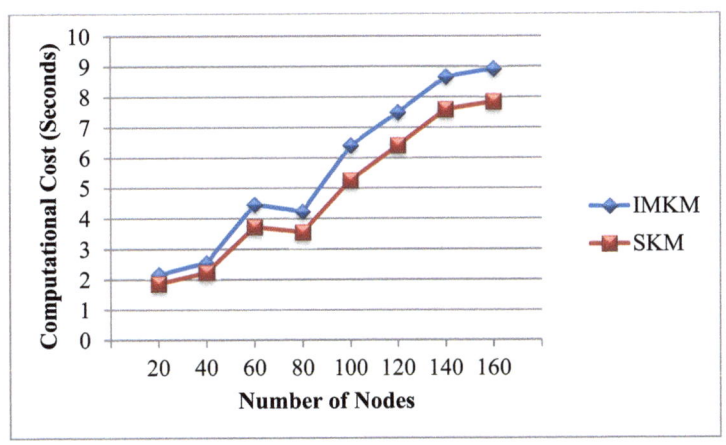

Figure 3.9 Computational Cost

The computational cost for the secure key model is shown in Figure 3.9 for different set of nodes including SKM and existing IMKM technique. Each node holds adjacent reputation records to determine the node's memory capacity, CPU power maintenance in updating records and other resource utilization.

Finally, secure key model facilitates secure communication in MANET with detection of malicious nodes using reputation and ranking. Experimental results shows that secure key model approach performs much better in terms of malicious node detection efficiency, node reputation, performance rate and computational cost compared to existing IMKM Scheme.

3.9 SUMMARY

The proposed secure key model facilitates secure successful communication between the nodes in the network without any loss of data. The reason behind packet loss is presence of malicious nodes. Malicious node detection efficiency is high (5 to 18% more) in proposed SKM compared to existing IMKM. Development of secure key model on the basics of level-based symmetric approach increases the node reputation by 9-21% when compared to existing IMKM. The reputation system proficiently determines the reputation value based on the threshold value. Moreover, the reputation value discards the unauthenticated node to involve in the communication increasing the security of the MANET. In order to enhance the lifespan of the network, the secret key is created and circulated by all cluster heads. In addition the proposed system supports high performance rate of about 5-9% in minimum computational cost in contrast to existing IMKM. Finally, SKM not only justifies the detection of malicious nodes, and also negotiates the node attack and communication failure providing a better way of secure communication.

CHAPTER 4

A HYBRID APPROACH FOR NODE CO-OPERATION BASED CLUSTERING IN MANET

4.1 INTRODUCTION

A MANET is termed as a set of wireless nodes built in infrastructure less environment with network services afforded by the nodes. In such a situation, if a node declines to co-operate with other nodes, then it will lead to a considerable diminution in throughput. MANET relies on the collaboration of nodes for packet routing ahead. Nevertheless, much of the existing work in MANET imagines that mobile nodes probably possessed by selfish users follows prearranged protocols without variation. Therefore, implementing the co-operation between the nodes turns out to be a significant issue. In the previous chapter a secure key model for ad hoc network with efficient node clustering based on reputation and ranking model is described. But the downside is that less co-operation with the nodes results in a communication error. Existing method termed as Fair, Efficient, and Secure Cooperation Incentive Mechanism (FESCIM) to stimulate the node cooperation in MANET fails in the process of identifying misbehaving nodes. FESCIM drops the packets due to mobility and bad channel. Maliciously and frequently dropping packets is a noticeable malicious behavior, causing less security.

A hybrid approach for node co-operation based clustering in MANET is proposed to avoid the security issues in MANET. The node cooperation among the nodes in MANET is enhanced by evaluating the weightage of cooperativeness of each node in network. The forecasting of node cooperation weightage is able to identify the illogical nodes participating in the network. Nodes are reconstructed on its own with the estimation of normal co-operative nodes. The reorganized nodes are clustered to avoid the frequent dropping of packets leading to secure communication among the nodes in the MANET environment. Experimental evaluations are conducted to confirm the efficient hybridization of node co-operation based clustering in terms of node cooperativeness, clustering energy dissipation and network lifetime.

4.2 NEED FOR NODE CO-OPERATION BASED CLUSTERING IN MANET

The need for the fast deployment of independent mobile users is a fact for next generation of wireless communication system. Major examples comprise starting survivable, well-organized, active communication for emergency or liberate operations, failure release efforts, and military networks. Such network circumstance does not depend on centralized and organized connectivity and is considered as applications of wireless ad hoc networks. A wireless ad hoc network is an independent group of mobile users that interacts over relatively bandwidth constrained wireless links. The set of applications for wireless ad hoc networks is different, ranging from small, motionless networks that are controlled by power sources, to large-scale, mobile, highly dynamic network which is shown in Figure 4.1.

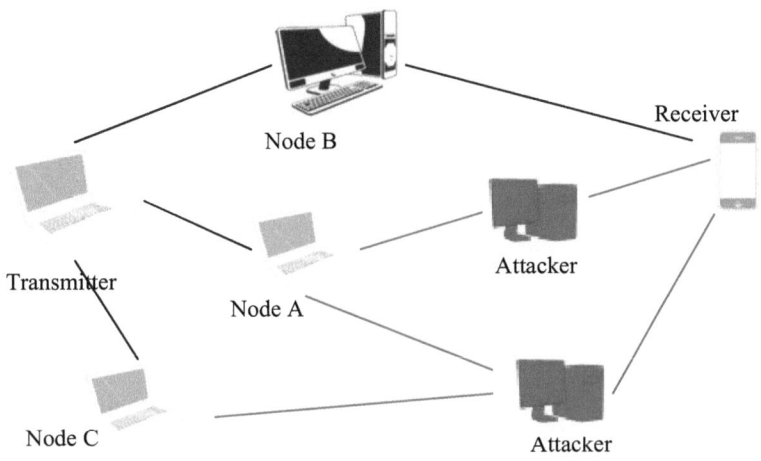

Figure 4.1 An Example of Wireless Ad Hoc Networks in Civilian Environment

Additionally, in a military environment, security, latency, reliability, intended jamming, and recovery from failure are important concerns. Military networks are considered to preserve a minimum possibility of intercept and a minimum possibility of detection. Hence, nodes choose to emit little power and broadcast infrequently to decreasing the probability of detection or interruption. A drop in any of these necessities possibly degrades the performance and reliability of the network.

Since the nodes are mobile, the network topology changes quickly and randomly over time. The network is decentralized, where all network behavior including determining the topology and distributing messages is performed by the nodes themselves, i.e., routing functionality is integrated into mobile nodes. The model of network protocols for these networks is a difficult issue. Despite the application, wireless ad hoc networks require significant distribution to decide network organization, link arrangement, and routing. Cooperation among nodes is very important in MANET. Without nodes broadcasting packets to other nodes, interaction over multiple hops is not feasible and the nodes stay disconnected. Thus, a stable contribution from all participants of a MANET is essential to maintain the nodes linked and thereby the network operational.

A MANET consists of mobile devices forming a momentary network without a preferred structure or central management. In a permanent network, nodes are linked by wires. They are fixed and have limitless energy. They possess more bandwidth compared to mobile networks. In mobile networks the nodes use radio transmitters instead of wires for interaction and nodes communicate through a fixed base station termed access point. Unlike in the previous networks forms, in most of the MANET network the major nodes function as a communicate node, transmitting traffic for other nodes in the network, and there is no fixed base station. The network only will operate if there is cooperation among the several nodes. If nodes do not cooperate, the possibility will survive that section of the network get inaccessible from the rest. So it is essential that there is cooperation without being too cruel for the nodes with low resources, like energy and bandwidth. This report gives a review of methods to stimulate cooperation between nodes in MANET and decides which of these are appropriate for clustering.

In a perfect network, the involvement of every node by broadcasting packets to the network is the identical and hence, equality is not a point of concern. Regrettably, nothing is ideal. There are always nodes which do not co-operate. They do not have the resources to participate in the network communication.

Enhancing the cooperation of the nodes in MANET communication is able to maximize the bandwidth of the network, because the improved connectivity of the network leads to more possible routes in the network. If more nodes are cooperating, the average number of packets that each node will be broadcasting will be highly reduced leading to lower energy consumption and more justice in the network.

4.2.1 Challenges of Node Cooperation in MANET

The MANET network not only conveys advantages, but also brings challenges. Believe that each node in a resident wireless MANET indicates an individual. There are numerous causes for a node to reject cooperation and avoid doing broadcasting other nodes packets. Also forwarding the packets engages transmission time, which the node cannot use for forwarding its own packets. Forwarding packets consumes battery power, which is an expendable resource on mobile devices. But, with uncooperative nodes interaction over multiple hops turns into unfeasible, as no packets are forwarded and the multi-hop ad hoc network stops to survive. Therefore, cooperation is one of the key issues in resident wireless MANET networks. The key is to stimulate the cooperation of nodes either by exhausting non-cooperative activities or by rewarding cooperative activity.

4.2.1.1 Mobility management

In contrast to infrastructure based networks, in ad hoc networks like MANET all nodes are mobile and is linked dynamically in a random manner. All nodes of these MANET perform as routers and participate in detection and preservation of routes to other nodes in the network. The mobility of the nodes in wireless ad hoc networks emerges two issues. The first is position of node in a MANET environment. Second, the updated information of nodes position in the network. Therefore, a node needs an identical recognition and some representations to broadcast and rescue position information of nodes. A centralized solution is available with hybrid approach. The clustering operation is capable of offering clear advantage over mobile ad hoc networks in maintaining the information of the nodes position. Energy efficient clustering and cluster head rotation scheme for wireless sensor networks was proposed by Ashok Kumar et al (2011). The proposal offers better clustering formation but it is time consuming and clustering energy dissipation is low. In addition, it faces the problem of large overhead in external information passing for cluster maintenance.

4.2.1.2 Power control and bandwidth allocation

Wireless hosts are generally powered by batteries which offer a restricted quantity of energy. Consequently, approaches to minimize energy consumption are of attention. One possibility to save energy is to employ power saving mechanisms. Power saving mechanisms permits a node to come into a dozen states by powering off its wireless network interface when deemed reasonable. Another possibility is to use power control schemes which correctly differs broadcast power to minimize energy consumption. In addition to supporting energy saving, power control is potentially be used to enhance spatial reprocess of the wireless channel. Various power levels between different nodes bring in asymmetric links. As a result, RTS and CTS are broadcast using the highest power level. Data and ACK are forwarded by means of the minimum power level essential for the nodes to interact.

In wireless MANET networks, the link level bandwidth act as a significant role in providing high QoS for peer-to-peer communication. If a peer-to-peer communication exceeds numerous hops in the link layer, then the bandwidth that is allocated to such communication will be decided by the facility of the restricted communication, usually, in order to offer QoS routing and be proficient to execute tasks such as admission control. In Peer-to-peer communications requested bandwidth is verified against the link layer bandwidth router-by-router to determine a possible and acceptable path. Consequently, QoS routing relies on the capability of the system in computing link layer bandwidth. The task is not a major problem in traditional wired networks, while it becomes challenging problem in wireless MANET networks due to the volatile nature of the network topological changes and as a result to the variable ability of link layer bandwidth. QoS routing algorithms for wireless MANET networks straightforwardly use bandwidth as the parameter to attain QoS routing and assume the link layer is capable of providing such bandwidth without considering the complexity of these assumptions. Bernasconi et al (2007) stated that, the MAC schemes for wireless ad hoc networks are not capable of providing QoS. Therefore, it is very essential to design techniques and tools to learn the effects on the QoS in providing security.

4.2.1.3 Privacy and security

The increase of wireless MANET network is predicted where hold of wireless access or wired backbone is not possible. Wireless MANET network does not have any predefined infrastructure and all network examinations are configured and produced on the fly. Thus, it is understandable that with lack of infrastructure facilities and vulnerable wireless link attacks, security in ad hoc network becomes intrinsic fault. Providing high security within MANET networking is challenging due to following reasons

The vulnerabilities in wireless MANET networks are abundant. The wireless medium permits passive attacks such as sniffing of information. This information is used by an intruder to execute an active attack. Due to the wireless communication, an intermediate node drops packets instead of broadcasting. An intruder also attacks the management protocols like routing, cooperation of the wireless MANET network, either irritating a disturbance or a breakdown of the provided services.

Nodes within roaming environment with link to common radio links easily involve setting up ad hoc infrastructure. But the secure communication among nodes needs the secure communication linkage to interact with the nodes. Before setting up secure communication tie the node should be sufficient to recognize another node. So node requires offering of unique identity and linked qualifications to another node. But distributed identity and qualifications require authentication and security so that validity and reliability of transmitted identity and qualifications cannot be queried by receiver node. Every node needs to be ensured that transmitted identity and qualifications to receiver nodes are not cooperated. Therefore, it is important to provide security architecture to secure MANET networking.

The above mentioned problem simultaneously leads to privacy problem. Basically, mobile node uses several kinds of identities and that differs from link level to user application level. Also, in mobile environment very often mobile node is not prepared to disclose the individual identity or qualifications to another mobile node from privacy point of view. Any cooperation identity directs adversary to generate privacy hazard to user device. Unfortunately, the current mobile principles do not offer any position privacy and in many situations exposing identity is usual to generate communication link. Hence, a flawless privacy protection is needed to connect the usage of MANET networking.

A main basis for the security difficulties reclines in the lack of a dependable verification of nodes. Although, base stations are obtainable in wireless MANET networks, many nodes do not have a straightforward single-router connection to network. In a communication session, it is thus essential to verify all nodes on the path within the wireless MANET network. But, with rising node mobility the organization and preservation of security sessions between nodes and the base station does not extent. Depending on the appropriate the security issues in wireless MANET networks are directly linked to the individuals in mobile ad hoc networks. Sadek et al (2007) proposed a protocol called a class of cooperative communication protocols with arbitrary N-relay nodes, which is based on Symbol Error Rate (SER) and allows secure routing in managed and open environments, where not all participants required to be authenticated in order to participate. A high security based approach is required to provide a better protection with all participants involving in the network.

In particular, Mani & Kamalakannan (2013) and Mahmoud & Shen (2012), introduced a virtual currency called nuglets. Every network node has an initial stock of nuglets. Either the source or the destination of each network connection use nuglets to disburse the relay nodes for broadcasting data packets. Packets forwarded by or delivered to nodes that do not have an adequate amount of nuglets are removed. The charge of source and destination is able to under estimate or over-estimate the packet price. In addition, the virtual currency schemes provide more fairness and the collaboration among nodes in reputation-based schemes.

4.3 HYBRIDIZATION OF NODE CO-OPERATION BASED CLUSTERING

A hybrid approach for node co-operation based clustering is efficiently designed for enhancing a secure communication over MANET by improving the node cooperativeness among the nodes in the network. The Hybrid Approach for Node Cooperation based Clustering (HANCC) comprises of three operations. The initial process is evaluating the weightage scheme of cooperativeness in the system. After evaluation of node cooperativeness weightage, the self organization of node is done. Finally, stage is to cluster the nodes based on weightage scheme and self organization for a secure communication.

4.3.1 Evaluation of Weightage of Node Cooperativeness

The implementation of node cooperation in MANET is elaborated. Recall that virtual currency schemes proposed by, Mani & Kamalakannan (2013) and Mahmoud & Shen (2012) provide more fairness and the collaboration among nodes in reputation-based schemes is better. The virtual backbone, called Virtual Grid Architecture (VGA) is utilized for performing the node cooperation in MANET. VGA comprises of a group of nodes, termed as CHs, which are selected based on an efficient eligibility condition as in reputation and ranking. As the network area is partitioned into fixed-size square zones, each CH is an indication of the collection of nodes within its square zone. Actually, VGA performs better compared to optimal clustering. Figure 4.2 describes the construction of VGA both in identical transmission ranges and variable transmission ranges of MANET.

Identical Transmission Range

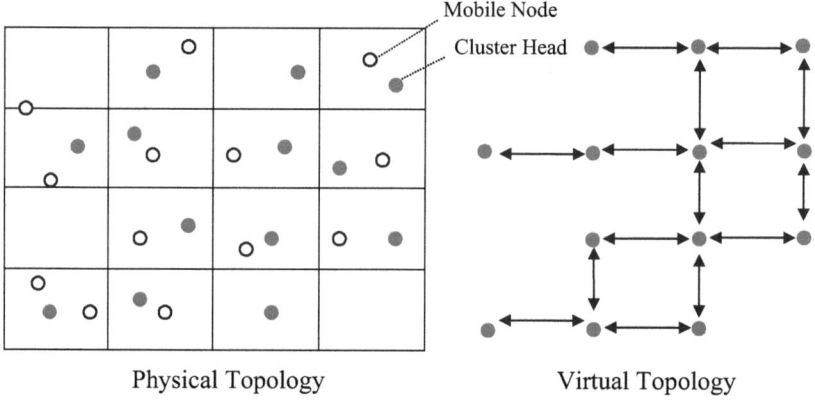

Physical Topology   Virtual Topology

(a) Homogeneous Networks

Variable Transmission Range

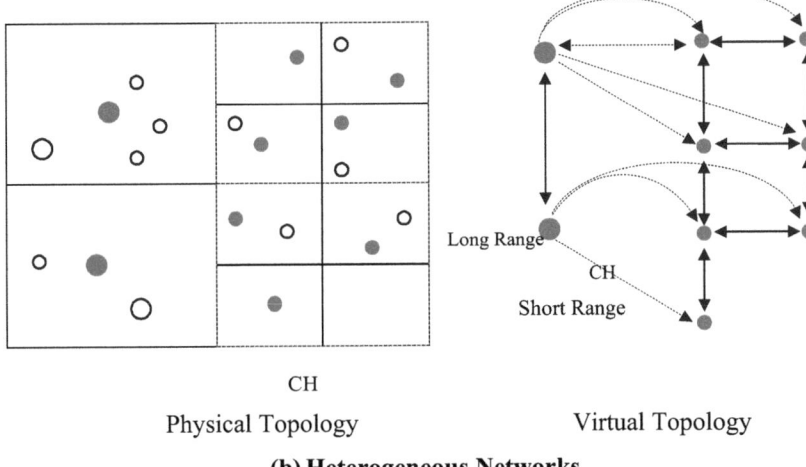

(b) Heterogeneous Networks

Figure 4.2 Construction of Virtual Grid Architecture

As shown in Figure 4.2, both identical and variable transmission ranges applied to homogeneous and heterogeneous networks. In the identical transmission, the selection process of cluster head is simple due to identical properties. Since the transmission range of each cluster is same that is they cover a fixed range in the cluster nodes which is shown in Figure 4.2(a). Figure 4.2(b) describes for variable transmission, here the CH selection is performed in two kinds; they are short and long range transmission nodes. Because in the variable transmission rage, the cluster head coverage area is not unique. The short and long range transmissions refer a function of a transmission power at the mobile nodes.

When a node comes into a new region of VGA, it transmits a message to recognize itself to the node in that region and to identify the neighboring nodes. Therefore, a node is able to recognize its neighbors. The model is constructed on Dynamic Source Routing (DSR) which in turn functions on top of VGA. In addition to this, each node in the network supports one of four categories of Reputation values (R). These are:

Fresh node: when a fresh node enters into the network for the first time, it is allocated with an initial value equal to 0

Regular node: it is a helpful node that has a reputation value R, $0 < R < E_s$

Excellent node: it is a helpful node that has a reputation value R, $R > E_s$.

Misbehaving node: a self-centered node that have a reputation value R, $R < E_m$

Here E_s and E_m are edge values for super cooperative and misbehaving nodes, correspondingly. The excellent nodes are required to represent the nodes in active participation than other nodes in motion.

In MANET, all nodes are conscious of the activities of all other nodes. Each node supervises the activities of its neighbor using a straight examination and a legitimate reputation message. Each node sustains a table that explains the activities of each of its neighbors. Each record in the table shows one neighbor and includes information regarding neighbor nodes like Entire Help (EH). EH is offered to other nodes in the network. When a source node A begins its session during a route of intermediary nodes, the first transitional node forwards the packet and all neighbor nodes increase the EH field connected to it by a value of one.

In addition, transactional node decrement EH for Node A based on the acknowledgment of the packet being send. If the intermediate node is declined by the packet then EH will be decreased by a value of two. The entire process is related to all nodes contributing in the forwarding function. Each node in the MANET needs to identify the weightage of cooperativeness with other nodes. The node cooperativeness is computed as shown in Figure 4.3.

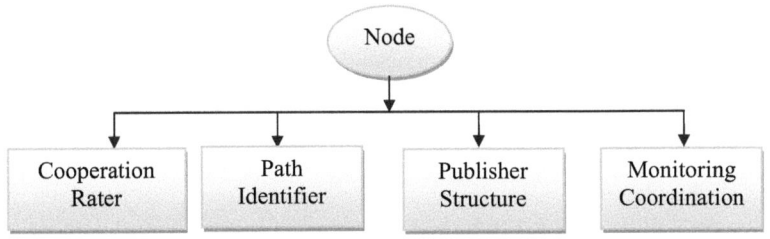

Figure 4.3 Computing Node Cooperativeness

The cooperation rater consists of

| Node Id | My Count | Node Entire Help | N or F |

Figure 4.4 Components of Cooperation Rater

Cooperation rater preserves each node in a data structure that illustrates the activities of its neighbors and some distant nodes. Each record in the data structure comprises the following information and it is mentioned in Figure 4.4:

Node ID: Distinct identifier of each node

My Count: Indicates the quantity of help given or received by the node

Node Entire Help: Entire help is provided to its neighbors by a node

N or F: denotes the neighbor (one-hop) node and distant node correspondingly

If there are several routes among the source and the destination, then the path identifier will choose the path with fewer probabilities for removing the packet. The publisher structure traces the ranking of the neighboring nodes. The publisher structure also practices all arriving reputation message in a definite node. Monitoring coordination observes the activities of its neighbors and reports to the cooperation rater. Using the cooperative rater, the cooperativeness of the nodes is computed reliably.

4.3.2 Process of Self-organization and Node Clustering Based on Cooperativeness

A system will be believed to be self organized, if it is organized without any peripheral or fundamentally devoted control entity. Each individual node communicates straightforwardly with other nodes in a peer-to-peer infrastructure. The ever-present interaction structure of MANET is appropriate to concern the intend principles of self-organization. The plan models the construction of self-organizing networks. Plans are local activity rules to attain universal characteristics, to develop understandable coordination, to reduce long-lived circumstances information and to devise protocols capable of any topology changes.

Use of limited information and least state information involves less communication overhead. It leads to openly decode into power efficiency. Thus, self-organizing design models is utilized to efficiently use the limited resources of the nodes in the MANET. The clustering scheme fulfilling the design model of self-organization helps to construct energy conserving and adjustable cluster models. The self-organizing design models and usefulness of self-organizing in further clustering operation are elaborated as follows:

4.3.2.1 Local activity rules to attain universal characteristics

Self-organizing design model attempts to share the task among the individuals. No single individual is responsible of the complete system in operation. The localized activity rules are utilized to all individual nodes. The localized activity rules repeatedly guide to the preferred universal characteristics. Self-organization model uses the information extracted from adjacent nodes to facilitate a fresh node in joining a cluster.

4.3.2.2 Development of understandable coordination

The main objective of self-organized clustering method is to provide better coordination. The hop count in the self-organization denotes the distance of the node from the cluster head.

4.3.2.3 Reduction of long-lived circumstances information

Clustering scheme utilizes a routing protocol within the cluster to preserve information on relationship of the cluster. This facilitates to reduce the long-lived circumstances information in self-organization. The cluster head in clustering formation is unnecessary to maintain additional information.

4.3.2.4 Protocols capable of any topology change

The cluster formation includes a routing protocol that is capable of any topological changes. Self-organized model is not controlled by any central control to begin the clustering. Additionally, the model does not require knowledge of the entire MANET and its topology to cluster the nodes. The cluster head does not engage latency in cluster formation. The clustering metrics facilitates in adjusting the formation of the cluster to its environment. When the nodes in a MANET are with high mobility then value is smaller as compared to the case when the nodes are stable. The self-organization of the nodes is performed after determining the weightage of the node cooperation.

After completion of computing the node cooperativeness, the self organization of nodes in MANET takes place. Since the node cooperativeness weightage is processed based on the activities, now the network environment consists only of true nodes by discarding the selfish nodes which involved in node attack, message lost and so on.

4.3.3 Clustering Based on Weightage and Self Organization of Nodes

The clustering of node is done based on the cooperativeness weightage. The clustering process is done based on the nodes which have high cooperativeness weightage and acts as a CH. After assigning the cluster head, the CH will manage to group the nodes based on the cooperativeness weightage matched with it. Then the communication takes place among the nodes based on clustered value. The process of the proposed hybrid approach for node cooperation based clustering is described in the following section.

The clustering formation proposed by Ashok Kumar et al (2011), faces the problem of large overhead in external information passing for cluster maintenance. The new self organized clustering scheme attempts to reduce the external information passing for cluster formation. Self-organizing and weightage based clustering uses the inter cluster routing information for cluster formation without the need for external passing of control messages. Minimizing the external control messages in the cluster formation and cluster maintenance phase facilitates power consumption of each node in MANET. This increases the lifespan of each node in MANET and hence of the network as whole. In node clustering the cluster head does not have any additional overhead of routing all packets of its cluster. Thus, the power consumption of the cluster head is the similar as that of any ordinary node inside the cluster. The cluster head in cluster formation avoids external information regarding the cluster.

Clustering of nodes based on weightage and self-organizing identifies the cluster gateway during cluster formation phase of the cluster. This minimizes the overhead by removing the explicit messages required to evaluate cluster gateways. Thus, clustering operation based on weightage of node cooperation and self-organization perform better in terms of information passing, power usage, latency in cluster formation and assignment of roles such as cluster head, cluster gateway, cluster member to the nodes in the cluster. Further self-organization handles the cluster head moves out of the cluster. A new cluster head is to be re-elected. Cluster head election process of VGA is based on the statement of cooperative environment. Cooperative environment involves all mobile nodes into communication toward the CH election process. A variance is emerged between local energy conservation and network operation when the cooperative situation is undisturbed, such as in the case of selfish users. The CH selection process considers and removes the node selfishness toward the CH election. Re-election of a cluster head in a partitioned cluster without degenerating node, the overall structure of the MANET in clustering process improves the security and QoS overcoming the limitations proposed by Sadek et al (2007) and Bernasconi et al (2007). Finally, the hybrid approach for node cooperation based clustering enhances the security level through forecasting weightage of node cooperativeness and increases network lifespan by self-organizing the nodes.

4.3.4 Node Clustering using HANCC

The first process is to evaluate the cooperativeness of each node in the MANET. The evaluation of cooperativeness is done based on the behavior and activities of the node done during the communication between the nodes. The monitoring of the behavior of the nodes is carried out and based on that the cooperativeness of the nodes is assumed. Monitoring is an entity that overseas nodes for evidence of misbehavior as well as good behavior and updates the reputation of the node accordingly. In MANET, it may not always be possible to appoint a trusted central agent for monitoring other nodes connectivity or availability of a central agent cannot be guaranteed. The authors proposed a monitoring scheme where the one hop neighbor of a node is responsible for monitoring the node.

The monitoring will be adapted with better observing ability where a neighbor waits for a time to overhear if the packet is transmitted. The reputation of the node is increased else the reputation of the node is decreased depending on the results of overhearing. The reputation is not altered every time a packet is dropped or forwarded but is recomputed periodically. Weightage of node cooperation is computed with the aid of monitoring schemes. The weightage of the cooperativeness of each node is computed based on the spatial events occurred at different aspects of communication.

The second process is self organization of nodes after computing cooperativeness of the nodes. The process of clustering is performed with the determination of normal co-operative nodes. Based on the weightage scheme and self organization of nodes the clustering operation is performed to offer security during communication in MANET environment. The Figure 4.5 describes the process involved in node clustering for secure communication using HANCC.

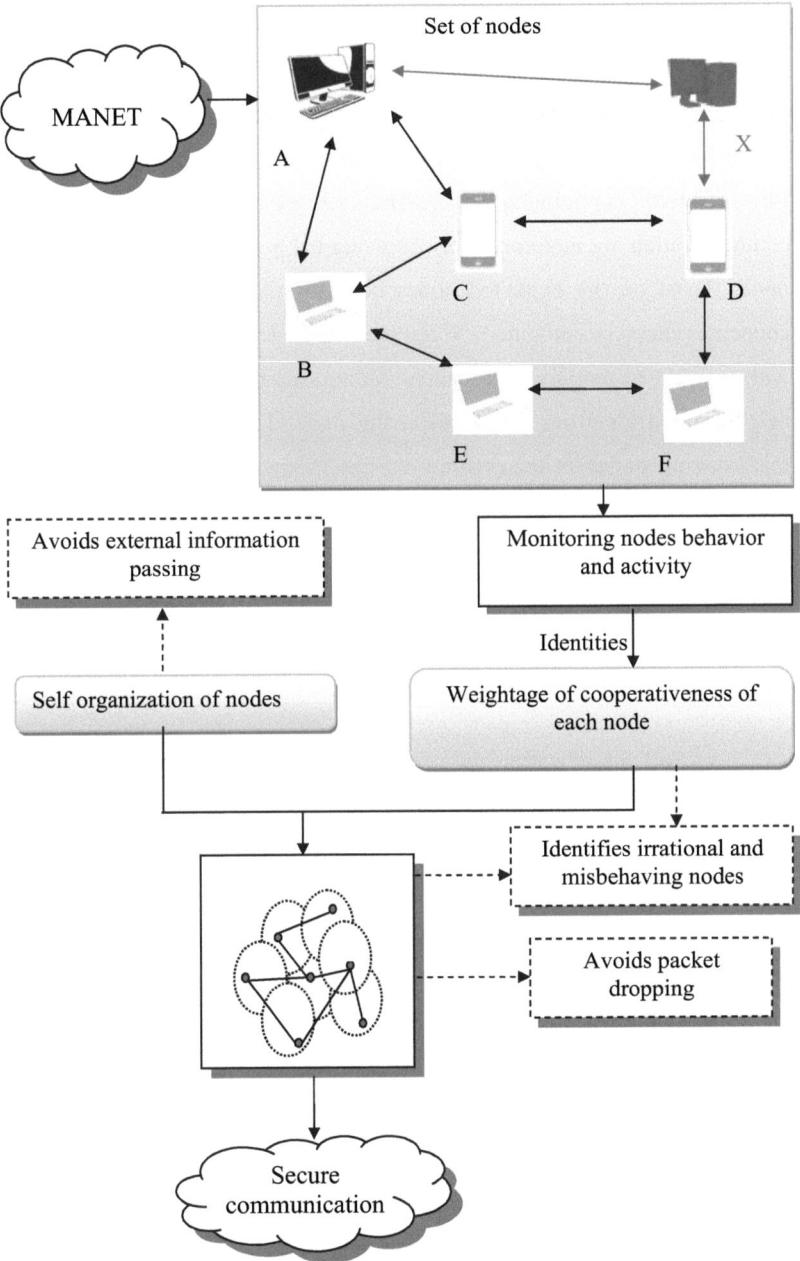

Figure 4.5 Node Clustering for Secure Communication using HANCC

Figure 4.5 describes the MANET consist of a set of nodes like A, B, C, D, E including the misbehaving node X. If the node X participates in the communication between the source and destination, there is chance for data packet loss. So, it is very important to form a cooperated and to secure cluster for effective communication. The set of nodes in the MANET communication are monitored for observing the behavior and activity of each node. Based on the extracted nodes behavior the weightage of the nodes cooperativeness is computed. Weightage of node cooperation is computed with the help of monitoring schemes. Monitoring by other good nodes in the neighborhood identifies the misbehaving node. The limitation of unnoticed misbehaving nodes in an existing a FESCIM is overcome by HANCC as monitoring operation in forecasting weightage of node cooperativeness identifies the misbehaving nodes. The weightage of the cooperativeness of each node is computed based on the spatial events occurred at different aspects of communication. The next process is to self-organize the nodes with the evaluation of normal co-cooperativeness of the nodes.

Self organization is one of the major concerns in MANET environment. After calculating weightage of the node cooperativeness, nodes self organize themselves to form a network of their own. The life span of the whole MANET network and the quality of the transmission is decided based on the network self-organization. Self organization of nodes with the clustering is useful for better formation of nodes and transmission. Since, clustering minimizes energy consumption by directing data from one node to another. After self-organizing of nodes, clustering of nodes is reorganized on its own. The reorganizing character of nodes in the form of cluster avoids unauthorized node to involve in the communication. In addition, the clustering of nodes leads a solution for a serious issue faced by FESCIM in identifying misbehaving and irrational nodes.

The final process is to cluster the nodes based on weightage scheme and the organization of nodes to provide a secure communication to the users involved in MANET environment. Clustering in MANET enhances the network operational performance. MANET faces serious difficulty in clustering as cluster formation is costly in terms of power deletion of nodes. The reason for high power consumption is the large number of message passed during the process of cluster formation. The difficulty in cluster formation is minimized due to the development of self-organizing principle for binding a node to cluster. The process avoids the external information passing in a cluster formation.

The node clustering depending on weightage scheme and self-organizing nodes are hybridized. Determination of the weightage and organization nodes is clustered causing a protection to the nodes. The clustering operation holds the packets more tightly before transmission. The clustering activity avoids the packet dropping due to holding of nodes in a group. Existing FESCIM drops the packets due to mobility, bad channel, maliciously and frequently dropping packets is a noticeable malicious behavior causing less security. The difficulty in FESCIM is sufficiently defeated by HANCC through the development of node clustering combining weightage scheme and self-organization.

4.3.5 **Algorithm for HANCC**

Input: Set of nodes N, message M

Step 1. For each node N

Step 2. Assign node ID

Step 3. Identify the activities of node

Step 4. Monitor the activities (B) of the node

Step 5. End for

Step 6. Note the path (P) chosen by the node from the beginning

Step 7. Note the total help (TH) provided by the node N

Step 8. For Each Node based on P, TH, B.

Step 9. Compute the weightage of cooperativeness (WC)

Step 10. End for

Step 11. For Each node based on WC,

Step 12. Reorganize the nodes in the MANET

Step 13. Cluster the nodes

Step 14. If WC (node) has max. Value

Step 15. Assign it as Cluster Head

Step 16. Cluster head manage the group by forming a nodes with better WC

Step 17. Form a group

Step 18. End if

Step 19. End for

Step 20. Stop the process

The process of the proposed hybrid approach for node cooperation based clustering is described elaborately in the above algorithm. For each node in the MANET, it is necessary to assign a node ID and to monitor the activities of the node. The path chosen by the node is also being noted to identify whether the node follows correct path to transmit a message. Then, the node is identified whether it can adjust with the behavior of other nodes in the network. After computing the weightage of cooperativeness, the reorganization of node takes place. Clustering is done based on the cooperativeness value and found the cluster head to form a cluster group to provide a secure communication for the nodes involved.

4.4 EXPERIMENTAL EVALUATION

The node cooperativeness estimation based clustering is efficiently done through evaluating the cooperative rater. To estimate the performance of the hybrid approach for node cooperation based clustering, the simulations on a Linux machine are run with P4-3.4 GHz processor and 2 GB of memory. A hybrid approach for node cooperation based clustering is implemented in an NS-2 environment. The simulation area extents 900 x 900 m^2, in which nodes can move from a random starting point to a random destination, with speeds of 3, 6, 9 m/s and a pause time of 3 to 5 seconds.

At first, the nodes cooperativeness is identified based on the behavior and activities of the nodes in the network environment, after evaluating the cooperativeness value, the nodes are reorganized in a same way. Then, the node clustering is done based on the maximum value obtained by the node in cooperativeness range. Since the node clustering is performed based on weightage of cooperativeness scheme, the clustering process becomes an efficient one. Then, the communication among the nodes is also being good compared to an existing FESCIM as proposed by Mahmoud & Shen (2012). Additionally, the clustering formation of weightage of node cooperativeness and self-organization is compared with energy efficient clustering and cluster head rotation scheme for wireless sensor networks proposed by Ashok Kumar et al (2011). The performance of the hybrid approach for node cooperation based clustering is measured in terms of node cooperativeness, clustering energy dissipation and network lifetime.

4.5 RESULTS AND DISCUSSIONS

The nodes cooperativeness is initially identified based on the behavior and activities of the nodes in the MANET communication with the evaluated weightage value of the node cooperativeness. Then, the node clustering is carried out based on the maximum value obtained by the node in cooperativeness range. The node clustering is done with the weightage of the node cooperativeness and self-organization. A hybrid approach for node cooperation based clustering is compared with existing model used by Mahmoud & Shen (2012), FESCIM to show high security and is compared with energy efficient clustering and cluster head rotation scheme for wireless sensor networks designed by Ashok Kumar et al (2011), to prove the efficient clustering.

4.5.1 Node Cooperativeness

Node cooperativeness describes the cooperativeness of the nodes in the network. In the HANCC, the node cooperativeness range is detected based on the behavior and activity of the node done till the communication with the other nodes takes place. Figure 4.6 describes the cooperativeness of the nodes after applying the FESCIM and HANCC method. The result of the hybrid approach for node cooperation based clustering is compared with FESCIM designed by Mahmoud & Shen (2012), for multi-hop cellular networks. FESCIM encourage minimum node cooperation in rational attacks.

Table 4.1 Node Cooperativeness

Number of Nodes	Node Cooperativeness (%)	
	FESCIM	HANCC
20	39	45
40	44	50
60	46	53
80	57	68
100	50	59
120	64	72
140	69	81
160	74	86
180	78	95

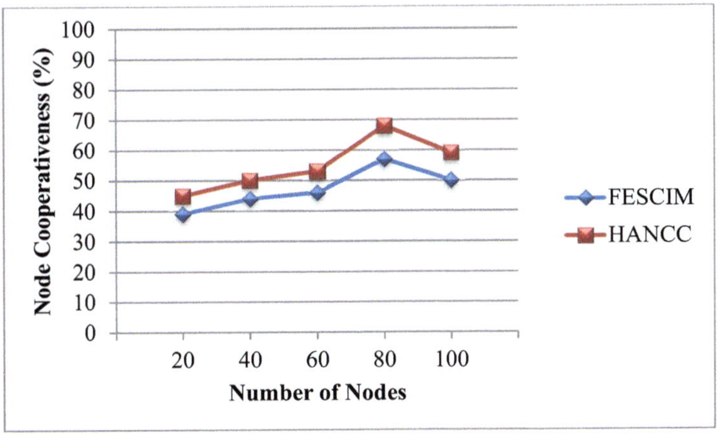

Figure 4.6 Node Cooperativeness

Figure 4.6 illustrates the node cooperativeness of each node involved in the MANET communication. HANCC provides high node cooperation of about 20-25% compared to FESCIM. As the node cooperation task is decided based on monitoring the nodes in communication.

4.5.2 Clustering Energy Dissipation

Minimum clustering energy needs extends the network lifetime and is used as parameter to demonstrate the efficiency of clustering. The node which has high cooperativeness range acts as a cluster head and the job of cluster head is to form a group based on weightage of cooperativeness range. The clustering efficiency is measured in terms of how the cluster group will process without allowing the misbehave nodes. Figure 4.7 describes the efficiency of clustering of the nodes after applying the ERP-SCDS and HANCC method. The result of the hybrid approach for node cooperation based clustering is compared with ERP-SCDS proposed by Ashok Kumar et al (2011).

Table 4.2 Clustering Energy Dissipation

Number of Nodes	Clustering Energy Dissipation	
	ERP-SCDS	HANCC
10	0.36	0.53
20	0.39	0.62
30	0.48	0.67
40	0.51	0.72
50	0.57	0.77
60	0.60	0.82
70	0.64	0.84
80	0.68	0.87
90	0.71	0.91

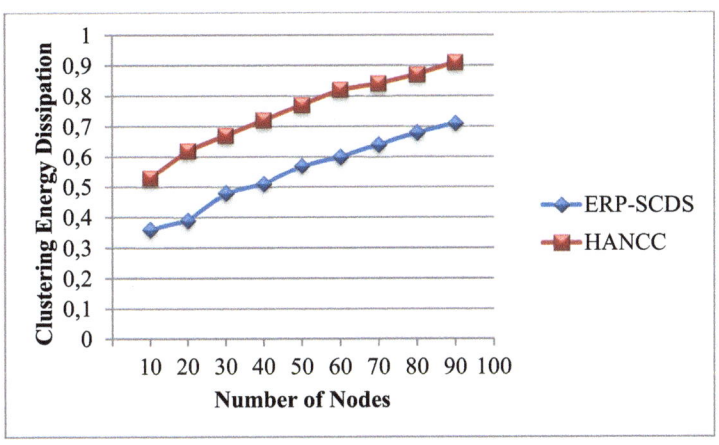

Figure 4.7 Clustering Energy Dissipation

Figure 4.7 describes the efficiency of cluster when the number of nodes increases in the network environment. ERP-SCDS is less efficient as it requires the location information transmission of every node to the sink only after receiving this information. Since in the HANCC, the node clustering is done based on the node cooperativeness range, and weightage measures, the clustering energy dissipation is high about 25-30% compared to energy efficient routing protocol for wireless networks with static clustering and dynamic structure (ERP-SCDS).

4.5.3 Network Lifetime

Network lifetime of MANET network is the time span from the forwarding packets in the path. Considering the number of nodes in MANET communication, the network life time is determined efficiently.

Table 4.3 Network Lifetime

No. of Nodes	Network Lifetime (%)	
	ERP-SCDS	HANCC
10	76	92
20	70	85
30	65	80
40	59	77
50	47	71
60	42	65
70	38	59
80	31	47
90	28	43

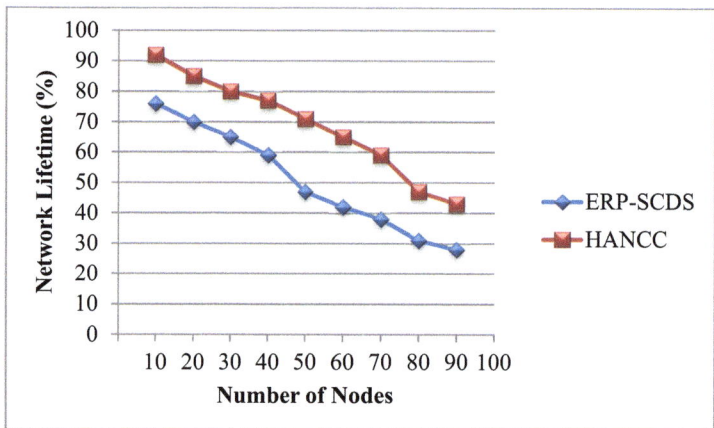

Figure 4.8 Network Lifetime

Figure 4.8 illustrates the network lifetime of each node involved in the MANET communication. Network Lifetime parameter is compared with HANCC and ERP-SCDS. HANCC provide higher network lifetime of about 15-20% compared to ERP-SCDS. Minimizing the external control messages in the cluster formation and cluster maintenance phase facilitates power consumption of each node in MANET. This increases the lifespan of each node in MANET in addition to self organization of nodes.

Finally, a secure communication is done based on the weightage of node cooperativeness range. Compared to an existing FESCIM model and ERP-SCDS the HANCC outperforms well even when attacker rate is high. The results describe the better performance of the HANCC. At last, it is being observed that the hybrid approach for node cooperation based clustering efficiently provides a communication framework among the nodes in the network in a secure manner by evaluating the nodes cooperativeness range.

4.6 SUMMARY

The study efficiently proved secure communication framework between the nodes in the network without any loss of data. Since the HANCC is based on the node cooperativeness range, the chance of loss of message is less. After estimating the cooperativeness range of each node, the reorganization of nodes takes place in its own. Then, the clustering of nodes is carried out efficiently and the chosen CH enhances transmission over the network. In order to enhance the lifespan of the network, node cooperativeness range is computed. Not only the malevolent nodes are discarded, which represent node attack and communication failure, but this also point to exceed the packet data in an efficient manner. Finally, the hybrid approach for node cooperation based clustering enhances the security level through forecasting weightage of node cooperativeness and increases network lifespan by self-organizing the nodes. The experimental results showed that the HANCC performs well in a secure communication over the nodes in the MANET network in terms of node cooperativeness of about 20-25% compared to an existing FESCIM model and ERP-SCDS.

CHAPTER 5

EFFICIENT NODE COOPERATION AND SECURITY IN MANET USING CLOSENESS TECHNIQUE

5.1 INTRODUCTION

A MANET does not wait on any eternal infrastructure. In description, all networking utilities nodes for routing and mobility management. Mobility management is accessed in a self-organizing manner. On the other hand, it is rigid to support cooperativeness among the nodes for their own restricted resources that require to be conserved. These scrupulous nodes which are also termed as selfish nodes decline to help other nodes in forwarding packets owing to the anxiety of saving resource. Several researches design a new method that aims at attaining confidentiality of the location for an efficient communication. The privacy appears from the mobile network and users expand the control over disclosure of their locations.

Bu et al (2011) designed, combined continuous user authentication and intrusion detection in high security mobile ad hoc networks using Value Iteration Algorithm (VIA) to provide security to MANET. But the value iteration-based solution for computing the Gittins Index only works for a MANET with a small number of nodes and states. For a large network with a variety of nodes, the value iteration based solution becomes computationally intractable and is inefficient in providing security to nodes. Another method proposed by Dong et al (2011), On-Demand Multicast Routing Protocol (ODMRP) using a High-Throughput metric (ODMRP-HT) is capable in providing high throughput but the efficiency in improving security in terms of quality is lower.

In this work, a closeness mechanism accepted from the assumption of small-world event or also termed as degrees of separation to persuade cooperativeness among nodes in a trusted node's community is proposed. The research work also provides some general idea on establishing a better security on the trusted MANET community by adapting security features of trust. The simulation of the proposed Efficient Node Cooperation and Security (ENCS) in MANET work is done for varying topology, node size, attack type and intensity with different pause time settings. The ENCS provide efficient node cooperation, clustering and performing closeness technique with large number of nodes. In addition, ENCS supports better security in MANET and outperforms well even when the numbers of malicious node are high. The performance evaluations are carried over in terms of packet transmission efficiency, average information leakage, average cost and security level compared with an existing VIA and ODMRP-HT.

5.2 VULNERABILITIES OF THE MOBILE AD HOC NETWORKS

MANET is infrastructure less network as defined before. Due to its structural characteristics, the mobile ad hoc networks are more vulnerable than the traditional wired networks. Security is a difficult task to preserve the packet in the MANET than in the wired network. The lists of various vulnerabilities that survive in the MANET are elaborated below.

5.2.1 Lack of Secure Boundaries

The sense of this vulnerability is self-evident. The vulnerability occurs due to unclear secure boundary seen in the MANET. The boundaries in the MANET network are compared with the plain line of protection in the traditional wired network. This vulnerability originates from the character of the mobile ad hoc network like freedom to attach, detach and travel inside the network.

In the wired network, intruders get physical access to the network medium, or even travel through several lines of protection such as firewall and gateway before inflicting malicious behavior to the destinations. But, in the MANET, there is no need for an intruder to obtain the physical access to stay in the network.

Once the attacker is in the radio range of nodes in the MANET, it interacts with those nodes in its radio range and thus joins the network automatically. As a result, the MANET is unable to offer secure boundary to protect the network from some energetic dangerous network accesses.

Lack of secure boundaries builds the MANET vulnerable to the attacks. The MANET undergoes all-weather attacks. The weather attacks force any node in the radio range of any node in the network at any time and aim to any other node in the network. The security of the MANET is affected more badly as there are various attacks endanger the network and make it even harder for the nodes in the network to defend against the attacks. The attacks generally consist of passive listening, active interrupting, data interfering, message repeat, and message corruption, denial of service and leakage of secret information.

5.2.2 Threats from Jeopardize Nodes Inside the Network

The previous subsection argues that the vulnerability due to lack of clear secure boundaries in the MANET leads to several link attacks. These link attacks lay their importance on the links between the nodes, and attempts to execute some malicious behaviors to make damage to the links. But, there are some other attacks that intend to increase the power over the nodes by some unrighteous means and then use the jeopardized nodes to perform additional malicious actions. This susceptibility is viewed as the threats that come from the jeopardized nodes inside the network.

Since mobile nodes are self-directed units that connect or disconnect the network with freedom, it is difficult for the nodes to execute some successful rules to maintain the feasible malicious activities from all the nodes it interact with. Because of the behavioral diversity of different nodes the transmission of packets is further difficult. Additionally, due to mobility nature of the ad hoc network, a cooperated node often modifies its attack goal and makes malicious activities to various nodes in the network.

Thus, it is very complex to follow the malicious activity executed by a jeopardized node particularly in a large scale MANET. Therefore, threats from jeopardized nodes inside the network are extreme and highly dangerous than the attacks from outside the network. The inside attacks are much complex to perceive as they come from the jeopardized nodes, which behave well before they are endangered.

A good example of inside attack threats comes from the possible Byzantine failures attacked in the routing protocol for the MANET. Byzantine failure occurs when a set of nodes are suspected in the network. The efficient node cooperation between the nodes in the ENCS is such a way that the inaccurate and malicious activity is straightforwardly detected.

Because of the cooperation among these suspected nodes, the execution of malicious activities are highly detected. The cooperated nodes apparently perform healthily. In addition, the cooperated node essentially utilizes the defects and variation in the routing protocol to gradually demolish the routing fabric of the network. The suspected node promotes new routing information that holds missing link, gives false link state information, or even floods other nodes with routing traffic. Because the suspected nodes are not easily recognized, their malicious activities are prone to be unobserved by other nodes. Therefore, Byzantine failure is very harmful to the MANET without node cooperation.

The above descriptions show that the threats from jeopardize nodes inside the MANET needs additional attention. Additionally, the trust on mobile nodes and infrastructure of any node in the network is undesirable even if it performs well before it is compromised.

5.2.3   Lack of Centralized Management Facility

MANET is an autonomous network without a centralized piece of management equipment such as a server. The unavailability of central piece of organization leads to some vulnerable problems.

First of all, the non-existence of centralized management equipment creates the detection of attacks a very hard problem as it is not simple to observe the traffic in a highly energetic and large scale MANET. It is quite frequent in the MANET that benign failures, such as path breakages, broadcast harms and packets dropping occur regularly. As a result, malicious failures are more complex to detect, particularly when adversaries alter their attack outline and their attack destination in various periods of time.

For each of the losses, as it can only monitor the failure that happens in it, this short-time examination cannot make a believable conclusion that the breakdown is caused by an attacker. But, quite simple to examine from a system point of view that the attacker has performed such a large quantity of misbehaviors that is securely conclude that all of the failures caused by this attacker should be malicious failure instead of benign failure. From this example, it can be concluded that lack of centralized management machinery causes various problems when the attacks in the ad hoc network is detected.

Secondly, absence of centralized management equipment blocks the trust administration for the nodes in the MANET. In MANET, all the nodes are needed to cooperate in the network process, as no Security Association (SA2) is understood for all the network nodes. Thus, it is not helpful to make an a priori classification, and as a result, the common attempt of establishing a line of resistance, which differentiates nodes as trusted and non-trusted, cannot be attained in the mobile ad hoc network.

Thirdly, some algorithms in the MANET depend on the cooperative participation of all nodes and the infrastructure. The lack of centralized management and decision making in MANET directs to decentralize, so the attacker make use of this vulnerability and present some attacks to crack the cooperative algorithm proposed by Guan et al (2012).

In one word, the lack of centralized management equipment reasons susceptibility that controls numerous features of operations in the MANET. An efficient technique is required to deal with the lack of centralized management problems.

5.2.4 Restricted Power Supply

Due to the mobility of nodes in the MANET, it is frequent that the nodes in the MANET depend on battery for the purpose of power supply method. While the nodes in the wired network do not depend on the power supply trouble as they receive electric power supply from the channels, which usually indicate that their power supply should be roughly unlimited. The nodes in the MANET necessitate considering the controlled battery power, which leads to several issues.

The primary difficulty caused by the restricted power supply is Denial-of-Service attacks proposed by Shu et al (2010). Since the attacker identifies that the destination node is battery-restricted, either it endlessly sends extra packets to the destination and requests it routing individuals extra packets, or it makes the destination to be fascinated in some manner of time-consuming calculations. By these, the battery power of the target node is consumed by these worthless tasks, and thus, the destination node is out of service to all the kind service needs as it has run out of power.

Additionally, a node in the MANET performs in a selfish way when it discovers that there is only restricted power supply. The selfishness reasons some troubles when there is a requirement for this node to cooperate with other nodes to hold some functions in the network. The difficulty in power restriction is considered in ENCS with the operational behavior of clustering neighboring nodes in monitoring node all time to observe the abnormal behavior in the network traffic for the entire cluster.

But, an important precondition for ENCS technique is that every node in the cluster is prepared to take their task in monitoring node and supply to all other nodes in a period of time interval. There are some nodes that perform selfishly and unlike to cooperate in the monitoring node selection process. The selection process becomes a failure on the presence of too many selfish nodes.

Furthermore, not all the selfish nodes are malicious nodes. Some nodes meet restricted power supply problem and thus behave in a selfish manner. The selfish behavior is tolerable but there are some other nodes that purposely broadcast it, runs out of battery power and so do not desire to cooperate with other nodes in some cooperative operation. But essentially, this node still has sufficient battery power to carry the cooperative operation. In a word, selfish behaviors should not be observed as malicious behaviors, but necessitate knowing if the selfishness is really caused by the restricted battery power, or by the intended non-cooperation. ENCS is planned in a way to affect DoS attack by eliminating selfish nodes.

5.2.5 Scalability

At last, the scalability problem is addressed in the list of vulnerabilities in MANET. Unlike the traditional wired network the scale is normally predefined when it is intended and the scale of the ad hoc network remains varying all the time. Because of the mobility of the nodes in the MANET, it barely calculates the number of nodes. As a result, the protocols and services that are functional to the MANET such as routing protocol and key management service are well-matched to the constantly varying scale of the MANET, ranging from decades of nodes to hundreds of nodes, or even thousands of nodes.

From the above discussion, it is concluded that the MANET is insecure by its nature. There is no such obvious line of resistance because of the freedom for the nodes to connect, disconnect and travel inside the network. Some of the nodes are compromised by the attacker and thus, make some malicious activities that are inflexible to detect. Lack of centralized equipment causes some troubles when there is requirement to have such a centralized administrator.

Restricted power supply leads to some selfish problems and incessantly varying scale of the network set higher needs to the scalability of the protocols and services in the MANET. As a result, compared with the wired network, the MANET needs more healthy security scheme to ensure the security of it. In the next section, ENCS elaborates the security solutions to security related problems and improves the security environment in the ad hoc network.

A MANET comprises of self-directed mobile nodes that are liberated to roam subjectively with no central controller for instance router to establish the communication paths. Each node in the mobile ad hoc network relies on each other so as to promote packets. This sort of MANET needs mobile nodes to contain good collaboration with each other to make certain that the commenced data communication process is a success. On the other hand, it is not simple to support cooperation as there are existing nodes with selfish behavior in the network.

The selfish behaviors on nodes are forced to protect their own partial resources for example battery energy, time and bandwidth in MANET. These nodes are very calculative as they use other nodes possessions for their broadcasts but hesitate to split their resources to assist other nodes processes. This phenomenon is common because there is no middle controller or essential authority in MANET.

In a wireless network, a communication range of node will frequently not face the whole network, so end-to-end transmission might require routing information during some nodes. So, ad hoc networks are termed as multi-hop networks, where a bound is a straight link among two nodes. In an ad hoc network, nodes are referred to as routers or terminals. Since ad hoc network is an environment without infrastructure, the co-operation among the routers is worst.

Since they are independent of each other, the problem might arise in the routing framework. The nodes are also being misbehaved. These types of nodes are referred to as selfish nodes, when selfish nodes in the network increases, then lifespan of the network will automatically decrease. The main solution to address these problems is secure routing.

Even though, the node's precision to remain its resources at fine performance for its individual data communication operation, where that type of activities will carry no good to the successful of MANET operation. For a particular node to drive or accept packets, the assistance of every connecting node is very vital. If all nodes in a distinct MANET environment perform selfishly, the outcome of such problem will guide to zero throughput.

In MANET, environments which rely seriously on nodes contribution, the reality of selfish nodes would involve the triumphant of a packet communication. Since the trouble is processed by the authoritative internal nodes, even with the consumption of the best cryptographic method will not resolve the problem. Thus, there is a requirement to propose a resolution that could promote the cooperation among nodes. MANET is typically self-organized networks and transitional nodes broadcast the uninterrupted communication. To attain this, each node depends on its neighbor to pass the packet to the target. In fact, most of preceding revises on MANET has absolutely unspecified that nodes are supportive.

As such, the concern of node cooperation becomes very imperative in MANET. Nevertheless, cooperation is made harder to implement in MANET than in communications based networks owing to numerous reasons.

At initial stage, nodes can subjectively connect or depart the network. Second, recognition of naughtiness and consequent separation of a misbehaved node has to effort in a dispersed method owing to lack of central control.

Finally, user precise requirements or approach should not be overlooked. Some users observe their power resource as being restricted by battery life, and consequently they may not believe disposed to transmit track for other users. As such, a user's performance will blow the system performance determined by his relevance needs or substantial constraints. This study presents a technique to diminish the trouble of containing selfish nodes in MANET known as closeness mechanism that is agreed from the premise of event to promote cooperativeness among nodes in a trusted environment.

5.3 ACHIEVING COOPERATION AMONG NODES

Cooperation among nodes in MANET is inflexible to be completed owing to the existence of self-centered nodes that do not desire to place their restricted resources like battery power, CPU and bandwidth at risks. It vigorously concerns them in a packet transmission operation. For instance, a selfish node merely crash packets that are anticipated to be thrower to other nodes as serving forwarding those packets disgraces its resource. The occurrence is obligatory in closeness technique since each node has its individual right to do so as there is no essential organizer in MANET environment to inform each node about the process of cooperation. Consequently, a network operation is paralyzed as MANET relies deeply on intermediary nodes to promote packets till end of process. Nevertheless, the cooperation between nodes in MANET is confident with the utilization of appropriate mechanism

Closeness technique from diminutive world event diminishes the selfish node's trouble effectively in MANET. The elimination of selfish nodes avoids the DoS attacks, a limitation, which was designed by Shu et al (2010). The closeness technique is processed by generating common trust between nodes before they enter the network path. The common trust among nodes is fashioned by enclosing physical associations in advance which are recognized along with the relationships prepared by a particular mobile node's in the network. Closeness technique presented a mobility replica depending on the association of mobile devices approved by individuals into the network. It represented the behavior of the nodes in the network by moving in groups that present a structure of relationships, therefore, capable to forecast the association pattern of nodes based on the decisions carried out by the trust values.

The same notion is processed in this closeness mechanism whereby the construction of relationships among nodes is done based on the communications made by the users who institute common trust with each other. All the nodes' relationship uniqueness will then be processed by individual nodes to create initial trust. Nodes that have been surrounded in the closeness mechanism are extremely cooperative with each other owing to the primary trust element that has been formed in advance.

By adapting ENCS mechanism, nodes are permitted to promote packets simply amongst trusted nodes in the group. As for that, nodes are not be able to assist other unidentified nodes that are not in the nodes trusted list as they are surrounded in the ENCS mechanism policy. The nodes are punished for being selfish owing to the opposition to cooperate with other nodes which are not in the similar group of nodes, but owing to they are appreciative to pursue the rules of the group nodes they are belong to, they are tagged as behave badly and therefore will not be punished. The careful forwarding activities such as transmit packets only among nodes are not only capable to avoid them from being punished but also set aside nodes' resources.

5.4   ENHANCING SECURITY OVER MANET

The closeness mechanism, though afforded a secure proposal for nodes to transmit with the organization of primary trust, is still facing some security threats particularly in managing compromised nodes. It is feasible for the neighboring nodes in the trusted list to be cooperated as there are many new security attacks. The security method by adapting features on every node symbolizes all nodes in the network with the evidence properties in the relevant nodes relationships organization process to produce a trusted MANET community. To accomplish security in MANET, numerous features are utilized. The security features are classified into two major categories namely performance metrics evaluation and quantitative trust value.

In performance metrics evaluation group, the effectiveness of chosen features utilized are accessed by employing definite metrics such as route detection time, routing traffic, routing overhead and number of data packets distributed. When a source node needs to promote packet to its destination, it requests its neighboring nodes to propose their feature's attribute number for inspection. If the neighboring nodes handle to present an attribute number that accomplishes the source node's constraint, the attribute number will be implanted in the packet format and the node is decided to promote the packet to other neighboring nodes earlier than attaining the vital destination. The effectiveness of packet forwarding process based on selected features are measured based on secure transmission from the source to destination in a less interval of time.

5.5 EFFICIENT NODE COOPERATION AND SECURITY IN MANET USING CLOSENESS TECHNIQUE

The ENCS work is efficiently designed for enhancing cooperatives of the nodes and secure communication over MANET by adapting the closeness technique. The ENCS method for node cooperation and security using closeness technique in MANET comprises of three operations.

Figure 5.1 illustrates the process involved in ENCS using closeness technique. The first process is evaluating the cooperativeness range of the nodes in the network. The second process is attaining the process of node cooperativeness in the network. The third process is to enhance the security of the nodes in the network.

The initial process in evaluating the cooperativeness of each node in the MANET is done based on the behavior and activities of the node done while the communication is taking place between the nodes in MANET. The monitoring of the behavior of nodes is carried out based on the cooperativeness of the nodes assumed. The weightage of the cooperativeness of each node is computed based on the spatial events occurring at different aspects of communication. The second process is to attain the cooperatives of the nodes in the mobile ad hoc network.

The third process describes about closeness technique that are able to motivate more cooperation between the nodes in a MANET environment. The closeness technique is adopted from the theory of diminutive world occurrence with six degrees of linkage. The process of recommending trust is carried on until each person attains the utmost level of the sixth degree of linkage.

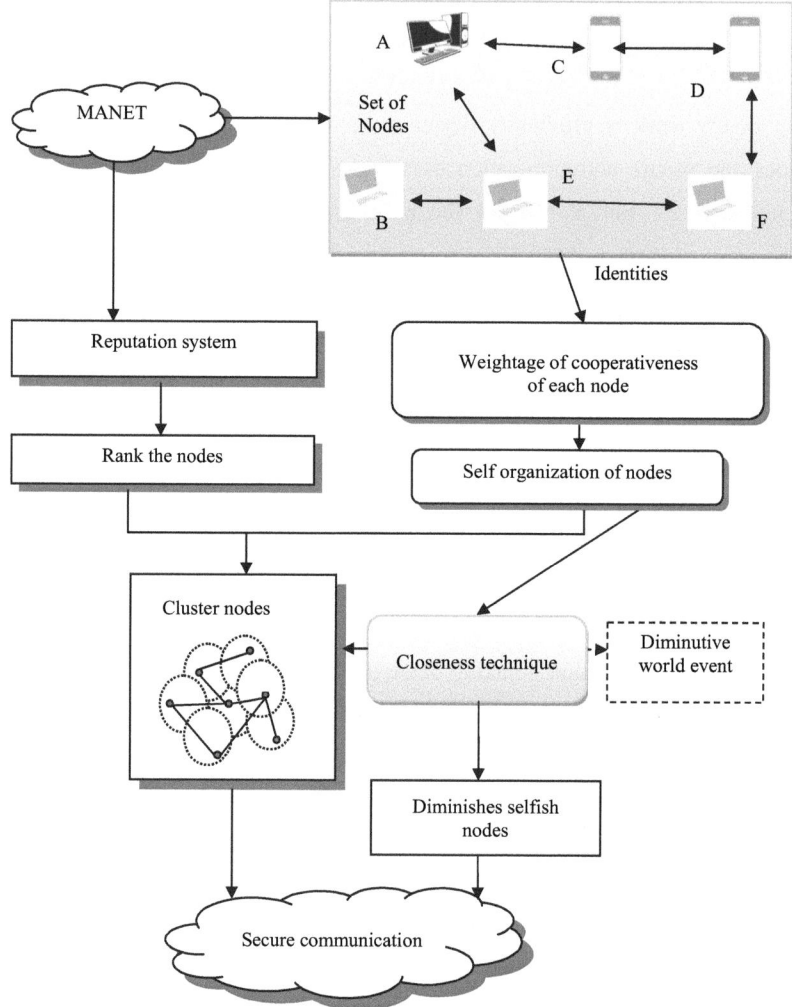

Figure 5.1 ENCS using Closeness Technique

Figure 5.1 shows that a clustering process is presented based on reputation and ranking system in an ad hoc network. The reputation system is enabled to allow nodes to construct informed choices regarding which nodes to assist with or prohibit from the network. To enhance the cooperativeness of the nodes, self organization of nodes is done harmoniously. For secure communication, closeness technique is presented to improve the security and cooperation of nodes in the network.

The expansion number of nodes is high, since the ENCS mechanism processes a unidirectional trust association as an alternative of bidirectional association. A unidirectional association reveals that a distinct node merely trust any node that it would similar to the situation of containing the entrusted nodes in the network. For instance, node A authenticate node B in a unidirectional method devoid of containing node B's approval. In unidirectional idea, this is measured as one preliminary trust association where as for bidirectional thought; node B must authenticates node A in return, only then one primary trust association is measured and created. The described notions can be further processed as shown in Figure 5.2 and Figure 5.3.

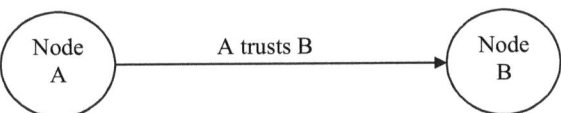

Figure 5.2 Unidirectional Relationship

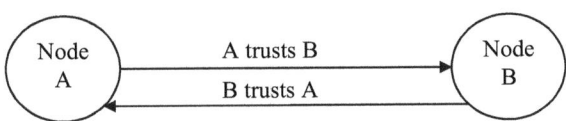

Figure 5.3 Bidirectional Relationship

Figure 5.2 show a unidirectional association to node B. The node does not surround trust to node A in return to generate a trusted association. Trusted relationship among the nodes is measured since, node A's right to authenticate either node it needs devoid of having to be trusted in return.

On the other hand, Figure 5.3 shows a bidirectional association needs of nodes A and B to authenticate each other so as to generate one trusted connection.

The idea of the ENCS mechanism is the recommendation of nodes around the network. The trusted value ranges in closeness technique increase the nodes cooperativeness of a trusted society. In security characteristic, even though the work does not affect any vital authority, the security is conserved in such a way that any two nodes are desired to contain a trusted value range before they launch a trust association with each other. The situation of closeness technique comes with the statement that all trusted nodes will not contain any disobedient property at all, because all involving nodes contain 100 percent reliability with each other.

5.5.1 Algorithmic Flow of ENCS Mechanism

Efficient node cooperation and security in MANET are found for varying topology, node size, attack type and intensity with different pause time settings. The ENCS mechanism algorithmic steps are shown below

Input: Nodes, $N_1, N_2, N_3, \ldots, N_n$, Threshold Value t, Reputation Table RT

Step 1. Start

Step 2. Identify best $t(N_n)$ node in MANET

Step 3. For each packet data,

Step 4. Check selfish nodes from N_n nodes

// **Reputation System**

Step 5. For each N_n

Step 6. Assign a rank $R(N_n)$ based on $RT(N_n)$

Step 7. Group the nodes N_n based on $t(N_n)$, R

Step 8. Choose the cluster head CH_i

Step 9. End for

//Closeness Mechanism

Step 10. For each node identify the weight W_i

Step 11. Cooperative node formation C_i

Step 12. End for

Step 13. For inspection

Step 14. Utilize feature's attribute number AN_i for validation

Step 15. Security feature selection (FS)

Step 16. Form a secure channel

Step 17. End for

Step 18. End for

Step 19. End

Output: Secure Node Cooperation in MANET

The above algorithm describes the reputation mechanism on the nodes N_1, N_2, N_3,...,N_n in MANET with threshold value t. The reputation system assigns the rank to the nodes based on most visited node i.e., the cooperation provides nodes. The selfish nodes are removed as on the checking process performed in the system. The similar numbers obtained in the ranking are grouped together in MANET. The grouped nodes based on rank are chosen as a cluster head CH_i.

The closeness mechanism in mobile ad hoc network forms a cooperative nodes C_i by removing the selfish behavior nodes. The set of nodes N_1, N_2,..., N_n identify the weight age for the cooperativeness of node formation. The inspections are performed on packet flow based on feature attribute number and validated by selecting the particular features to form a secure channel. The closeness mechanism developed an effective cooperativeness and secure channel in MANET.

5.6 PERFORMANCE EVALUATION

The node cooperativeness estimation and security using closeness technique are efficiently done through evaluating the cooperative rater. To estimate the performance of efficient node cooperation and security in MANET, simulations are run on a Linux machine having a P4-3.4GHz processor with 2GB of memory. ENCS efficient node cooperation and security in MANET implemented in NS-2 environment. The simulation area extents 900x900 m^2, in which nodes move from a random starting point to a random destination, with speeds of 3, 6, 9 m/s and a pause time of 3 to 5 seconds. At first, the nodes cooperativeness is identified based on the behavior and activities of the nodes in the network environment using closeness technique, after evaluating the cooperativeness value, the nodes are reorganized in a same way.

Then the node clustering is done based on the directional trust range values of the neighboring nodes. Since the node clustering is performed based on weightage of cooperativeness scheme, the clustering process is an efficient one. Then, the communication among the nodes is also being good compared to an existing secure key model framework. The performance of the efficient node cooperation and security in MANET is measured in terms of, average information leakage, packet transmission efficiency, security level and average cost.

Average information leakage rate during transmission of packets is defined as the data exposed and is compared with existing model proposed by Bu et al (2011). The level of cooperation extended by the node towards the MANET functions removes the misbehavior of selfish nodes increasing the security level. Node cooperativeness means that a node must not behave selfish in mobility model. This behavior speeds up the movement of nodes inside the network enhancing security. The security level is defined as the amount of security given for the fulfillment of an obligation using closeness mechanism (i.e.) the information flow from the source to destination in mobile ad hoc network system. It is measured in terms of percentage (%). The security method by adapting features on every node symbolizes all nodes in the network with the evidence properties.

Packet transmission efficiency is defined as the method of network data transmission, in which small blocks of data, or packets, are transmitted over a channel in mobile ad hoc network using the closeness mechanism. Transmission of standardized packets of data over transmission lines rapidly with high-speed switching enhancing the transmission time taken compared with ODMRP-HT designed by Dong et al (2011). Average cost denotes the number of packet transmission between the source and destination.

5.7 RESULTS AND DISCUSSION

ENCS method shows how a secure communication is done based on the closeness technique for node cooperativeness range. Bu et al (2011) proved that the existing structural results for combined continuous user authentication and intrusion detection in high security mobile ad hoc networks provides Value Iteration Algorithm (VIA) security to MANET. But the value iteration-based solution for computing the Gittins Index only works for a MANET with a small number of nodes and a small number of states and observation states. For a large network with a variety of nodes, the value iteration based solution become computationally intractable. The ENCS provides efficient node cooperation, clustering and performing closeness technique with large number of nodes.

In addition, ENCS supports better security in MANET and outperforms well even when the numbers of malicious node are high. The efficiency of ENCS is compared with the existing ODMRP protocol using a High-Throughput metric as ODMRP-HT designed by Dong et al (2011). Even though ODMRP-HT provides high throughput, the efficiency in providing security in terms of quality is lower. The results describe the performance of the efficient node cooperation and security in MANET.

5.7.1 Average Information Leakage

Average information leakage is defined as the rate of revealing information during broadcasting or extraction of information by the adversary. Average information leakage is avoided to a certain level by performing clustering formation bonding the nodes tightly causing less leakage of information. VIA provides less information leakage for a network but faces computational complexity in executing large number of nodes.

Figure 5.4 describes the tabulation for average information leakage. The results also show that the average cost and the average information leakage decrease when the number of available nodes in the network increases from 0 to 100. The reason is that there are more nodes that are selected for authentication and interruption detection, so suspected and low-energy nodes are avoided. Figure 5.4 shows that information leakage remains stable for the first four probabilities and decreases when the system becomes more secure in ENCS. The reason for this is that the ENCS avoid choosing the selfish nodes through closeness technique. When the closeness probability further increases, the average information leakage decreases.

Table 5.1 Average Information Leakage

Total Number of Nodes	Average Information Leakage (MB)	
	VIA	ENCS
20	8.06	7.58
40	44.15	43.18
60	11.18	10.22
80	12.55	13.16
100	36.25	35.23
120	20.46	19.95
140	23.91	21.14
160	28.54	22.78
180	34.21	26.25

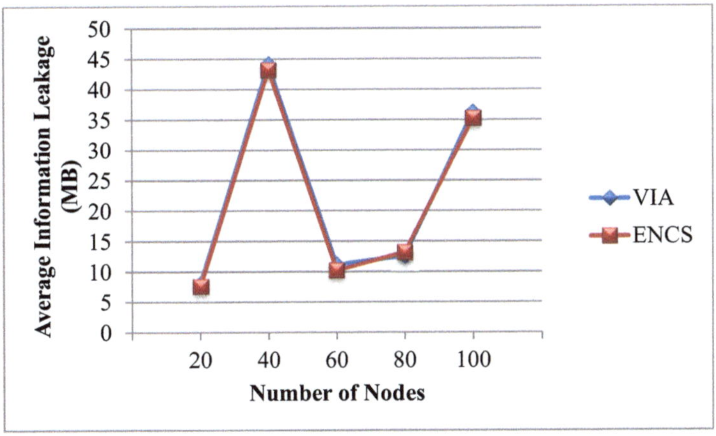

Figure 5.4 Average Information Leakage

5.7.2 Packet Transmission Efficiency

The packet transmission efficiency is measured based on the time required to process the incoming packets from source to destination. Packet Transmission

Efficiency (PTE) measure the performance of packet delivery using the closeness technique, defined by Equation (5.1)

$$PTE = \frac{DPT_{noattack} - DPT_{attack}}{DPT_{noattack}} \qquad (5.1)$$

DPT indicates the Data Packet Transmission. DPT_{attack} and $DPT_{noattack}$ represent DPT when the network is under attack and not under attack, respectively. Thus, data packet transmission efficiency captures the cost (number of data packet transmissions) per data packet received.

Compared to the existing ODMRP-HT, the ENCS consumes less time to transmit the packet. Since the ENCS presented closeness technique, the trust value of the neighboring nodes are estimated. Based on the trust values, the packets are passed to the nearest nodes in the network.

Figure 5.5 describes the packet transmission efficiency required to broadcast the packets from source to destination in a specified time. The results of the efficient node cooperation and security in MANET are compared with an existing ODMRP-HT (ODMRP protocol with high throughput). ENCS provides better data transmission efficiency with the given number of packets for about 10-15% compared to ODMRP-HT. As source node promotes packet to its destination as per the request of neighboring nodes features attribute number based on inspection.

Table 5.2 Data Transmission Efficiency

Number of Attackers	Cost per received Packet (pkts)	
	ODMRP-HT	ENCS
1	2.61	3.03
2	2.59	2.97
3	2.56	2.92
4	2.49	2.88
5	2.46	2.84
6	2.43	2.79
7	2.37	2.72
8	2.34	2.66
9	2.31	2.59

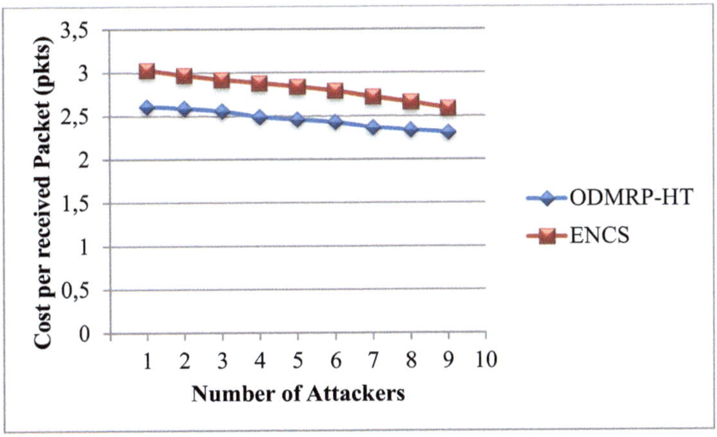

Figure 5.5 Data Transmission Efficiency

5.7.3 Security Level

ENCS facilitates high security on estimating the neighboring node trust values. Based on the trust values, the levels of security are recognized. Quantitative trust value inspected using the features attribute number aids in identifying the threats and the security levels which is computed using the Equation (5.2).

$$Security\ level = \frac{Quantitative\ trust\ value_{Feature\ attribute}}{Neighboring\ node\ trust\ value} \qquad (5.2)$$

ENCS is compared with the value iteration algorithm in structural results for combined continuous user authentication and intrusion detection in high security MANET proposed by Bu et al (2011). Figure 5.6 is depicted for both VIA and ENCS.

Table 5.3 Security Level

Number of Nodes	Security (%)	
	VIA	ENCS
10	40	56
20	42	61
30	46	67
40	49	70
50	54	74
60	58	78
70	62	81
80	68	86
90	74	91

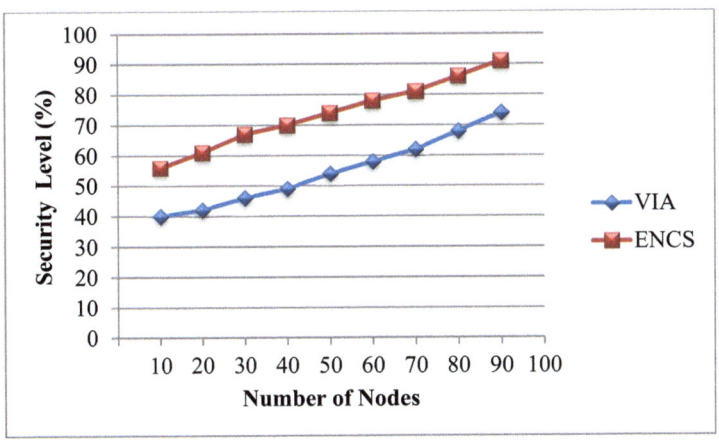

Figure 5.6 Security Level

Figure 5.6 illustrates the security level, compared to existing VIA, the ENCS has high level of security and the variance is 15-25% high. Since the ENCS supports security by estimating the neighboring node trust values leads to identification of security levels.

5.7.4   Average Cost

Average cost is defined as the number of packets transmitted per unit time. Existing VIA results in high cost since the other sensors make decision based on out-of-date Gittins indices. ENCS aims at increasing the average cost of transmitting data packets.

Figure 5.7 describes the average cost for the given number of nodes. Since the nodes in the reputation table makes better decisions with complete information, the average costs for packet transmission is increased. The results show that the average cost from the value iteration algorithm is less about 10-15% compared to ENCS.

Table 5.4 Average Cost

Number of Nodes	Average Cost (kbps)	
	VIA	ENCS
10	4.23	5.02
20	4.45	5.12
30	4.67	5.24
40	4.79	5.35
50	4.87	5.47
60	5.05	5.56
70	5.17	5.69
80	5.23	5.78
90	5.31	5.84

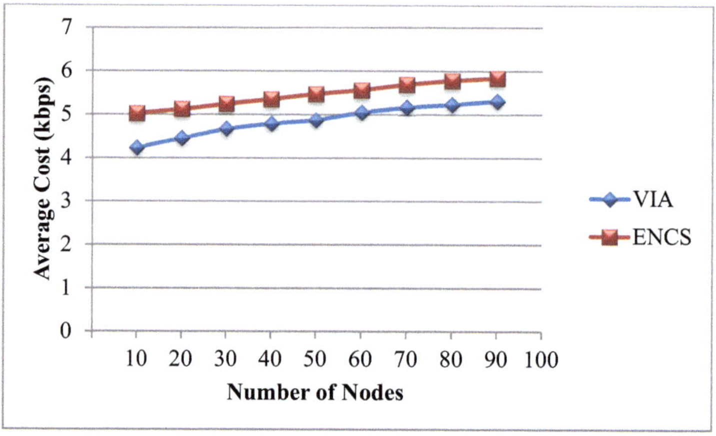

Figure 5.7 Average Cost

At last, the experimental evaluation concludes that the efficient node cooperation and security in MANET proficiently provide a communication framework among the nodes in the network in a secure manner by evaluating the nodes cooperativeness range.

5.8 SUMMARY

ENCS mechanism overcomes the bottleneck of selfish nodes in MANET by creating initial authentication among nodes through node cooperation. The ENCS mechanism is capable of providing high security by avoiding the misbehavior nodes from replacing the security associations with unidentified nodes. Security associations are only replaced with nodes in trusted community, improving the security inside group of trusted nodes. Security associations presented the realization of features in every node inside the group. The selections of security features are done based on the validation of common usage of nodes in the specified network. Experimental results showed that the ENCS mechanism outperforms in terms of packet transmission efficiency, average information leakage, average cost and security level in the range of 15-25% high compared to the existing VIA and ODMRP-HT.

CHAPTER 6

PACKET RESERVING AND CLOGGING CONTROL VIA ROUTING AWARE PACKET RESERVING FRAMEWORK IN MANET

6.1 INTRODUCTION

Mobile nodes communicate with each other using wireless channel where transmissions take place with significant interference. To expand a high-performance mobile ad hoc network, a key step is to develop scheduling algorithms. More specifically, scheduling algorithm stops a subset of connections with respect to the known network state information to avoid unwanted interruptions and network collisions.

Wireless medium is a shared resource, which is used by all nodes in the network. Throughput measurement, efficient controlling of the access to insufficient resource is a complicated task. Resource management schemes in mobile ad hoc network play a chief role in achieving the task. Packet reserving is one such resource management scheme which controls the allocation of bandwidth among multiple flows through node cooperation. Packet reserving focuses in solving the problems associated with multiple sessions, within a single node, shares the wireless link.

Position-based Opportunistic Routing (POR) protocol proposed by Yang et al (2012) takes benefit of the stateless possessions of geographic routing and transmits to the wireless medium. When a data packet is sent out, some of the neighbor nodes have overheard and the transmission will be offered as forwarding applicant. The concept of in-the-air backup considerably enhances the robustness of the routing protocol and decreases the latency and duplicate forwarding source by local route repair.

In actuality, due to the broadcast environment of the wireless medium, a single packet transmission will lead to multiple responses. Single packet transmission is used as it considerably enhances the strength of the routing protocol. The perception of such multicast-like routing strategy has already been established in opportunistic routing. Conversely, most of them use link-state style topology database to decide and prioritize the forwarding candidates for resource management. In order to acquire the inter node loss rates, periodic network-wide measurement is requisite, which is unrealistic for mobile environment.

As declared, the batching used by Yang et al (2012) and Bu et al (2011), proved that protocols also has a tendency to delay packets and is not preferred for much delay sensitive applications. Recently, location-aided opportunistic routing honestly uses location information to direct packet forwarding. Conversely, just similar to the other opportunistic routing protocols, it is still measured for static mesh networks and focuses on network throughput. The robustness bring upon by opportunistic forwarding has not been well explored for packet reserving.

Continuous user authentication and intrusion detection in high security as described by Bu et al (2011) are used to solve the security problem for a large network with a variety of nodes. Distributed continuous user authentication and intrusion detection scheduling problem fails to consider more node's states in making the reserving decisions in MANET.

Network partitions can occur regularly, since nodes move generously in a MANET, causing some data to be often inaccessible to some of the nodes. Therefore, data accessibility is repeatedly a significant performance metric in a MANET. Data are typically replicated at nodes, other than the innovative owners, to increase data accessibility to handle with recurrent network partitions. In universal, replication concurrently improves data accessibility and reduces query delay, query response time, in a MANET. Mobile nodes together have adequate memory space to hold together all the replicas and the creative data.

Joint topology control and authentication design in mobile ad hoc networks with cooperative communications is formulated by Guan et al (2012), as a discrete stochastic optimization problem. Discrete stochastic optimization does not necessitate prior faultless channel status and channel estimation. Topology control and authentication design fails to deal with the imperfect routing knowledge and dynamic changing topology. To achieve this, reserving scheme holds the challenging task such as changing topology, multi hops and shared wireless medium in mobile ad hoc network. In this work, route aware concept is explained to have the knowledge of route conditions. The condition refers to the quality of the channel which measured in terms of suitable metrics.

Route conditions in wireless networks are broadly classified as local and end-to-end route conditions. For mobile ad hoc networks, local and end-to-end routing is different. The difference between the local and end-to-end routing information is better understood by considering their typical characteristics. Local routing information considers four categories as frequency monitoring of the route state, granularity of route state, accuracy and measured-time with respect to packet delivery.

Typical parameters are used to represent the local route information such as established signal strength, signal-to-noise values, queue-length, burst-error mode, packet losses, and single hop delay and link lifetime. Whereas, parameters that perhaps symbolize the end-to-end channel conditions are path lifetime, end-to-end packet delay and queue length at each node.

In proposed work, focus is made on end-to-end route awareness and represents the end-to-end route quality in terms of path lifetimes. Routing Aware Packet Reserving (RAPR) framework is developed in MANET that takes into account both the clogging state and the end-to-end throughput maintenance. RAPR is complimentary system for packet reservation that utilizes only the local routing information available in each cluster. RAPR framework local routing information contains the node clustering, cooperation and high security level, which provides the maximal throughput among the contending flows. Further, simulation results show that minimal delay count and maximal throughput.

During the path setup in RAPR, estimates of the path lifetimes are collected and stored. The path lifetime value is used as a parameter to symbolize the end-to-end routing by controlling the clogging. During packet reserving, RAPR selects packets, which has high probability of reaching the destination, and takes into account the cost of a link. The break gives priority to flows that have a longer regularize with path residual lifetime backlog queue.

6.2 KEY IDEA BEHIND ROUTING AWARE PACKET RESERVING FRAMEWORK IN MANET

RAPR framework key idea is to represent end-to end route quality in terms of throughput maintenance. The network security level reflects the current end-to-end route state. The route state keeps changing continually which has temporal interval for which they are valid. RAPR defines the time interval for which the path associated for a flow of packets. If the time taken to perform each and every link of path 'Q' from node 'i' to node 'j' is estimated as $d_1, d_2, d_3, \ldots, d_n$ then the delay time will be,

$$Q_{i,j} = \min(d_1, d_2, d_3, \ldots, d_n) \qquad (6.1)$$

Path 'Q' delay time value is computed using Equation (6.1), and the packet reserving is performed with shortest path travel earlier approach. Shortest path earlier approach selects the packets which traversed for shortest distance, so that the remaining packets are reserved. The remaining packets lifetime is typically obtained using inference technique which incorporates with local route information.

A packet flow, along with its start and end times, is also defined by its divide-line and continuous period in RAPR framework to identify the packet transfer rate with effective resource utilization. A divide-line is the duration of time during which an attempt is made to transmit a packet from source to destination mobile nodes. RAPR framework frequently uses the divide-line in MANET to handle the packet reserving. The continuous episode denotes the time during which the flow receive the packet service. It is to be noted that after a continuous episode, the source pauses for some time and start transmitting on a different path with next reserved packet. Therefore it is important for all the packets of a flow to reach its destination successfully before the end of continuous episode.

For any specified moment of time, RAPR deal with single value of divide-line and continuous episode for any given flow, as RAPR have information about the node clustering route, node cooperation and security level values. Using the local route information RAPR framework, packet queued at the intermediate node reach the destination after the continuous episode.

6.2.1 Packet Reserving on Mobile Nodes

Each packet flow 'i' in RAPR running through a path is described with tuples $\{R_i, D_i, b_i, t_i, s_i, l_i\}$. R_i is the least amount of packet inter arrival time, D_i is the highest amount packet transmission time over a link. b_i and t_i are begin and end of the episodes of a packet flow. Finally s_i and l_i are the sets of continuous duration between the link and divide-line episodes respectively. s_i and l_i represent single continuous episode of packet flow 'i'. The relationship among s, l is illustrated in the course of Figure 6.1.

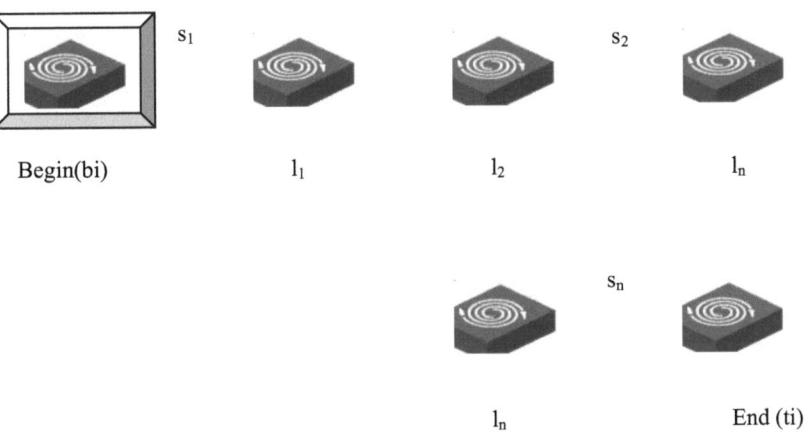

$s_1, s_2, \ldots, s_n$ - Continuous Duration between the Link
$l_1, l_2, \ldots, l_n$ - Divide line Episodes

Figure 6.1 Continuous Episode of Packet Flow in RAPR

Figure 6.1 illustrates the continuous flow of the packets from beginning to end of the mobile nodes with intermediate node links. RAPR span of a packet flow 'pf' is the interval {b, t}. The packet flow 'pf' served within this span. Let's define a packet reservation example 'E', as a sequence {pf$_1$,pf$_2$,...pf$_n$}. Formally a packet for E is seen as a function H, which is defined as

$$G : R \to \{pf_1, pf_2, ..., pf_n\} \cup \{\varphi\} \tag{6.2}$$

where, G (p ⊆ security-span (pf$_n$)) = pf$_n$. That is, nth packet flow is served at time p. Further G (p) = φ means no packet flow is being served. At moment p$_i$, a packet belongs to flow 'pf' receives a service (G (p$_i$) = pf) at any of the mobile nodes. The service at the one before the last node is performed, and then the packet transferred end to end with maximal throughput. Further, to denote the pending state of any packet flow 'pf', indicating the amount of workload remaining to be served for the queue at any time moment 'p', at any node, defined residue of flow as γ (pf, p).

The important optimizing factors in RAPR framework is defined as the amount of packets that remain in the network at the end of their respective continuous episode of all the packet flows. The amount of packets that remain in the network defines the resource utilization of RAPR framework.

$$\sum\nolimits_{i=1}^{n} \gamma\left(i, S_i^p\right) \tag{6.3}$$

$$\sum\nolimits_{i=1}^{n} pr(i) \tag{6.4}$$

where, $pr(i) = \gamma(i, s_i^p)$. s_i^p is the sets of continuous duration between the link at time 'p'. For each packet flow, the reserved packets gains the merit, based on the number of completely served packets. Packets which do get transmitted for a few hops get transmitted to the intermediate nodes for the merit of the effective resource utilization in MANET. The RAPR design a framework, which over an episode attains maximum throughput and minimum delay time, and also fairly distributes the achieved throughput among all flows. Minimizing delay time served in two purposes where, initial work it reduces the delay and second, it reduces the loss due to link breakages.

6.2.2 Single RAPR Model with Multiple Packet Flows

RAPR consider a simple model with multiple flows over a single bottleneck link. After the single shared link, these flows use different links with different resources.

RAPR assume a routing packet reserve form which schedules these packet flows T_i. Let us consider a single continuous episode o of "n" flows, with arrivals within this continuous episode, and no further arrivals. That is, RAPR takes a single snapshot in time of 'n' flows with each flow having single continuous episode of varying durations. For simplicity, let all flows have same R = 1, and D = 1. Therefore, T_i reserve the packet in s_{max} period, where s_{max} the maximum continuous episode of packet is flow and o_i represents the number of packets existing for packet flow 'i'. The maximum number of packets existing in all the queues is,

$$o_{sum} = \sum_{i=1}^{n} o_i \qquad (6.5)$$

Let call this value as o_{sum}. Therefore, percentage ratio of throughput would be $\frac{o_{max}}{o_{sum}}$. Now, adopt a fairness criterion, where ratio is maintained across all the flows. In other words, the throughput measurement is proportionately distributed across all the flows. The idea here is that all RAPR treated fairly by assigning the proportionally equal throughputs. That is, for each flow i, the throughput received is

$$Throughput\left(packet\ flow\ i\right) = o_i * \frac{o_{max}}{o_{sum}} \quad (6.6)$$

The rationale behind Equation (6.6) is based on the argument that shorter continuous episode of flows are merely due to the inherent property of ad hoc networks. Therefore, penalizing packet flows follows the inherit properties of the local route network. The local route network follows the clustering of nodes which is reorganized on its own self with the evaluation of normal co-operative mobile nodes. The node clustering prohibits unauthorized node to engage in the communication between the nodes in ad hoc network. The reorganized nodes are clustered to avoid the frequent dropping of packets leading to secure communication among the nodes using local route inherit properties in RAPR framework.

6.3 OVERVIEW OF ROUTING AWARE PACKET RESERVING FRAMEWORK IN MANET

RAPR reserving framework for mobile ad hoc networks takes into account local clogging information and end-to-end throughput information. RAPR begin with describing the importance of considering route awareness in general and delay in particular. RAPR formally defines the problem and describes the approach to resolve the effective resource allocation based on node clustering, node cooperation and higher security level. The overall diagram of RAPR framework is shown in Figure 6.2.

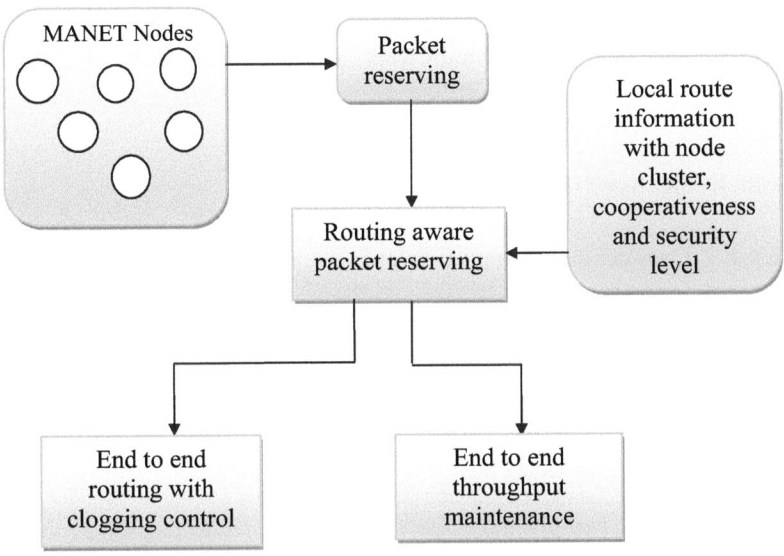

Figure 6.2 Overall Diagram of RAPR Framework

Figure 6.2 describes, set of nodes in mobile ad hoc network containing the packet for processing. Initially, packets are reserved using the routing aware packet reserving. The packet reserving in RAPR framework uses the local route information. The location route information for packet reserving is based on the node clustering, cooperativeness and security level. RAPR framework uses the routing quality to attain the end to end route information with clogging control and maximal throughput maintenance.

6.3.1 Algorithmic Description of RAPR Framework

RAPR considers end to end routing condition represented as enhanced network lifetime for route awareness, and also included a queue size parameter to make the scheduling scheme with clogging control. The combination of parameters avoids the clogging and reduces the accumulation of packets at the end of flow on time. A single queue with multiple packet flows is maintained in RAPR framework, and described through algorithmic flows.

Begin Packet Reserving in RAPR

Step 1.   Consider the set of packets 'pk'

Step 2.   From set of 'pk' packets formulize

Step 3.   Select the queue for packet reserving, such that for every queue q = TRUE in local routing mobile nodes

Step 4.   If clogging occurs then

Step 5.   Fails to perform end to end routing

Step 6.   Else

Step 7.   End to end routing performed with node clustering, cooperation and security factors

Step 8.   End If

Step 9.   Follow the shortest path travel earlier approach in RAPR

Step 10. Attain maximal throughput from source to destination mobile nodes.

End

RAPR performance varies as the accuracy of link inference varies. A set of packet flow in mobile nodes attains the end to end throughput maintenance through RAPR framework. The notion of packet reserving takes RAPR framework to make the effective resource utilization decisions for given values. Further, neighbor management and packet reserving list scheme in RAPR attains the security level with minimal cost average.

6.4 EXPERIMENTAL SET-UP OF RAPR FRAMEWORK

Packet reserving in mobile ad hoc network via routing aware packet reserving framework is evaluated using NS-2 to estimate the performance. The RAPR framework is evaluated in an efficient manner using 0 to 45 nodes in an area of 950 * 950 m^2. The nodes' incoming time (sec) is noted as t1, t2,...,tn. The resources are allocated effectively from node '1' to 'n' nodes.

The simulation results show that it takes 750 seconds to transmit the packet securely from source to destination by choosing the path (i.e.,) route efficiently. During the simulation, 40 nodes were contributed in the process. For evaluation purpose, the network topology is generated by NS-2 compared RAPR against joint topology control, authentication design, continuous user authentication, and intrusion detection.

In the simulation initially 40 clients were taken. Each node plays again one user's outline composed from synthetic data sources. In addition, some of the request sections of normal surfers are identified and played again to compute the delay time. The interval between two continuous requests is determined depending on three samples namely counting stable routing, growing rate of routing and arbitrary pulsing routing.

Simulation experiments are conducted with the set of mobile nodes using RAPR framework, Joint Authentication and Topology Control (JATC) scheme in mobile ad hoc networks and Partially Observable Markov Decision Process (POMDP). Simulation experiments are performed on the factors such as network security, communication overhead, end to end throughput rate, resource utilization efficiency, average cost and delay measurement based on node count.

Network security level is evaluated using NS2 simulator. It is defined as the provisions and policies adopted by a RAPR framework to prevent and monitor unauthorized access, and misuse of packet flow. RAPR involves in securing a computer network infrastructure. Communication overhead factor is a measure of the additional workload incurred in a RAPR algorithm due to irregular communication between the mobile nodes of the system.

RAPR end to end throughput factor defines the rate of successful packet delivery over a communication channel. Packet may be delivered over a logical link through a certain network node. The throughput is usually measured in Mega bits per second (Mbits/sec) based on node count. Resource utilization using the RAPR is the use of a resource in such a way that increases end to end throughput level. The RAPR aim is to use these assets efficiently so as to maximize user service levels. Average cost factor generally measured in terms of milliseconds is equal to total cost divided by the number of packets produced to the destination using the RAPR framework. Delay measurement after performing the test is defined as the amount of time interrupted when compared to the accurate simulation time, measured in terms of seconds.

6.5 PERFORMANCE OF RAPR FRAMEWORK

Routing aware packet reserving framework in MANET is matched to the existing joint authentication and topology control scheme in mobile ad hoc networks and partially observable markov decision process for performing the simulation result comparison. The various graphs describe the RAPR Framework improvements with beneficial end to end throughput compared with existing system.

Network security level is measured in JATC scheme, POMDP and RAPR framework. Security level varies with different schemes, measured in terms of percentage (%).

Table 6.1 Network Security Level

Techniques	Network Security Level (%)
JATC scheme	85
POMDP	89
RAPR framework	94

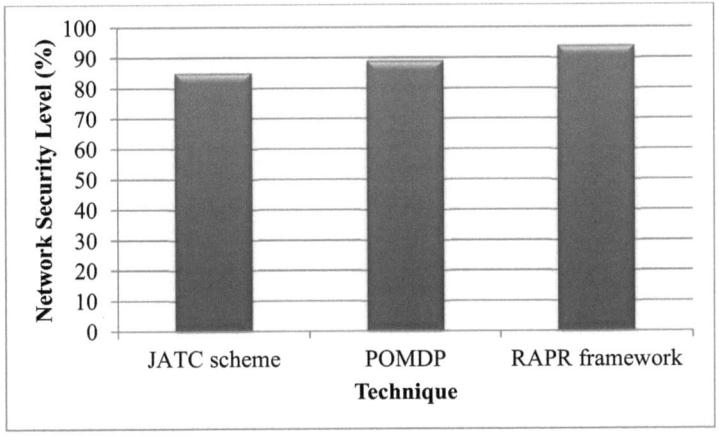

Figure 6.3 Measure of Network Security Level on Various Techniques

Figure 6.3 describes the security level in mobile ad hoc network. The network security level reflects the current end-to-end route state in RAPR framework. The route state keeps changing continually which has temporal interval for which they are valid. In RAPR uses the security span to improve the security level when the packets transferred from source to destination. In RAPR, n^{th} packet flow is served at time p and increases the security percentage by 5 when compared with the POMDP proposed by Bu et al (2011). At moment p_i, a packet belongs to flow 'pf' receives a service (G $(p_i,)$ = pf) at any of the mobile nodes, so the security percentage is also improved by 9 when compared with the JATC scheme designed by Guan et al (2012).

The JATC scheme, POMDP and RAPR framework overhead in NS2 simulation result is measured in terms of Bits per Second (bps). As the node count increases, communication overhead is reduced in RAPR framework when compared with the existing system.

Table 6.2 Communication Overhead Measure

Number.of Nodes	Communication Overhead (bps)		
	JATC scheme	POMDP	RAPR framework
2	610	517	505
4	753	678	650
6	867	771	722
8	592	512	491
10	633	552	525
12	547	495	470
14	647	568	537
16	758	675	632

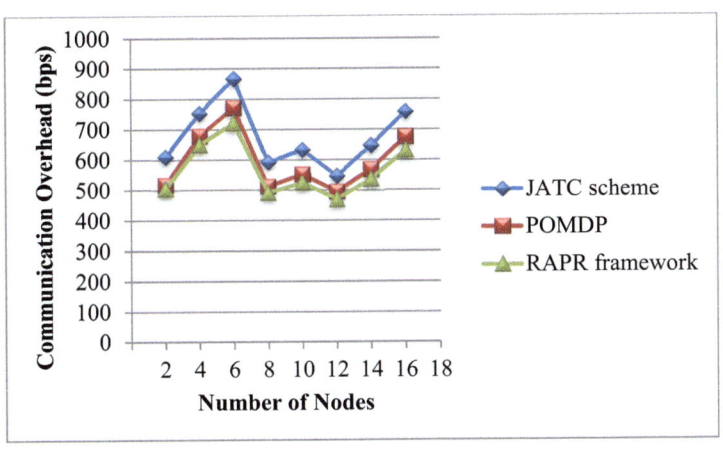

Figure 6.4 Measure of Communication Overhead

Figure 6.4 depicts the communication overhead on varying node count. Shortest-path-earlier-approach selects the packets which traversed for shortest distance, so that the remaining packets are reserved. The packet reservation makes the RAPR framework to communicate effectively with reduced overhead measure when compared with the JATC scheme, POMDP. The remaining packets lifetime is typically obtained using inference technique which reduces the overhead by 13 – 17 % when compared with JATC scheme 2 – 6 % reduced when compared with the POMDP.

Table 6.3 End to End Throughput Rate

Node Count	End to End Throughput Rate (Mbps)		
	JATC scheme	POMDP	RAPR framework
5	6122	7127	8137
10	5722	6131	7137
15	6167	7175	8189
20	6149	7154	8167
25	4940	5151	6164
30	5597	6216	7233
35	7124	8129	9151

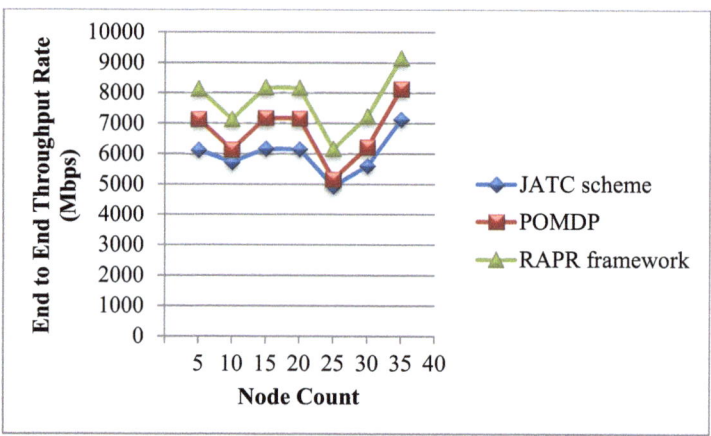

Figure 6.5 Performance of End to End Throughput Rate

Figure 6.5 illustrate the end to end throughput rate based on the node count. The packet reserving in RAPR framework uses the local route information. The location route information for packet reserving is based on the node clustering, cooperativeness and security level. RAPR framework uses the routing quality to attain the maximal throughput maintenance with

24 – 32 % higher when compared with the JATC scheme and 12 – 19 % higher when compared with POMDP.

Table 6.4 Resource utilization Efficiency

Number of users	Resource Utilization Efficiency (%)		
	JATC scheme	POMDP	RAPR framework
10	81	75	85
20	71	69	76
30	66	60	70
40	76	74	80
50	79	75	83
60	91	87	95
70	87	81	92

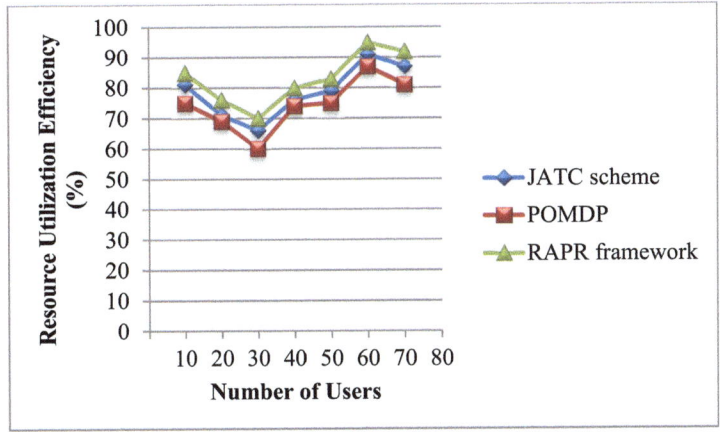

Figure 6.6 Resource Utilization Efficiency Measure

The resource utilization is measured based on the user group in mobile ad hoc network. A packet flow, along with its start and end times by its divide-line and continuous episode in RAPR framework identifies the packet transfer rate with effective resource utilization. A divide-line is the duration of time during which an attempt to transmit a packet from source to destination mobile nodes with effective resources.

The resource utilization in RAPR is effectively managed using Equation (6.3) and Equation (6.4) Where, $pr(i) = \gamma(i, s_i^p)$. s_i^p is the sets of continuous duration between the link at time 'p'. RAPR is 4 – 7 % increases resource utilization when compared with JATC scheme and 8 – 16 % improved when compared with POMDP.

The average cost of the JATC scheme, POMDP and RAPR framework using simulation result and average cost factor is measured in terms of milliseconds (ms). As the simulation second varies from 100 to 700, average cost varies gradually for every simulation seconds. Simulation result shows that the average cost is reduced in RAPR framework when compared with the JATC scheme and POMDP. Average cost measures the amount of overall packets flow through all the mobile nodes, within minimal time.

Table 6.5 Average Cost

Simulation Seconds (sec)	Average Cost (ms)		
	JATC scheme	POMDP	RAPR framework
100	224	218	212
200	223	214	192
300	421	390	360
400	91	88	83
500	510	480	443
600	219	203	187
700	365	343	315

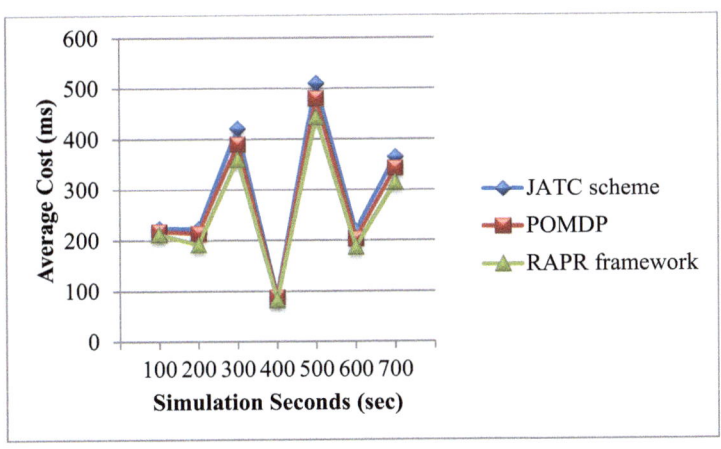

Figure 6.7 Measure of Average Cost

Figure 6.7 illustrates the average cost based on simulation seconds. RAPR assume a routing packet reserve form which schedules these packet flows T_i. T_i reserve the packet in s_{max} period which reduces the average cost in RAPR. Therefore, penalizing packet flows follows the inherit properties of the local route network, which reduces the average cost by 5 – 14 % when compared with JATC scheme and 2 – 10 % reduced when compared with POMDP.

Table 6.6 Delay Measurement

Node Speed (m/s)	Delay Measurement (sec)		
	JATC scheme	POMDP	RAPR framework
20	123	105	92
40	54	44	42
60	441	410	385
80	510	478	426
100	171	166	151
120	89	75	68
140	315	270	245

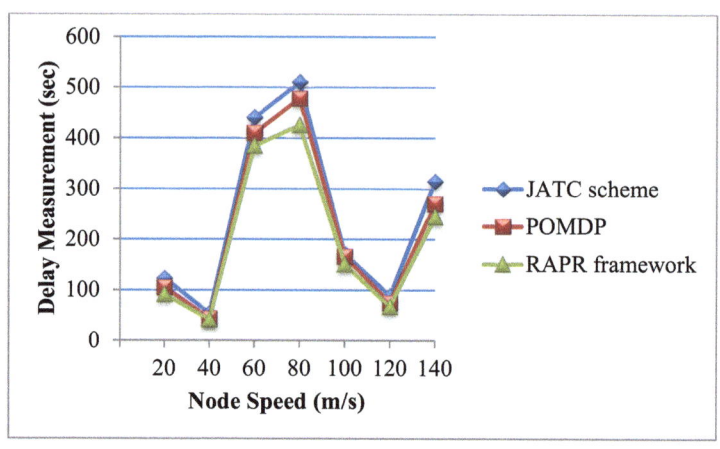

Figure 6.8 Measure of Delay Measurement

Figure 6.8 describes the delay count based on the node speed. Node speed is measured in terms of meter/seconds (m/s) and delay count measured in terms seconds. RAPR define the time interval for which the path associated with packet flows. If the time taken to perform each and every link of path 'Q' from node 'i' to node 'j' is estimated as $d_1, d_2, d_3, \ldots, d_n$ then the delay time will be measured in RAPR using Equation (6.1). The reorganized nodes are clustered to avoid the frequent dropping of packets leading to minimal delay in RAPR when compared with JATC scheme, POMDP.

RAPR framework reduces delay count by 11- 25 % when compared with JATC scheme and 4 – 12 % lesser when compared with POMDP. Finally, RAPR framework uses the local route information for effective throughput maintenance on mobile nodes using the node clustering, cooperation and security level. Therefore, penalizing packet flows follows the inherit properties of the local route network with minimal delay time.

6.6 SUMMARY

Routing aware packet reserving framework in MANET considers the end to end routing condition with maximal throughput. RAPR is a complimentary system where the packet reserve utilizes local routing information. The local routing holds the information of the node clustering, node co-operation and security level. RAPR follows the approach of shortest path travel earlier approach. The mobile nodes select the packet which travels in shortest distance earlier from the queue to reduce the delay count. Path setup in RAPR estimates the security level of the system, and symbolizes the end-to-end routing by controlling the clogging. RAPR reaches the packet to the destination with high probability ratio and minimal delay count. Simulation results attain the maximal network security level, end to end throughput rate and resource utilization efficiency. On the other hand, simulation result also reduces the communication overhead, cost and delay time in RAPR framework. Finally, RAPR designed to perform effective resource utilization with 15.3% improved end to end throughput maintenance.

CHAPTER 7

CONCLUSIONS AND FUTURE WORK

7.1 CONCLUSIONS

The secure key model facilitates secure successful communication between the nodes in the network without any loss of data. The security of the communication is better in the secure key model with the operation of reputation system, ranking in node clustering and group key agreement protocol. The reputation system expertly determines the reputation value based on the threshold value. The reputation value rejects the unauthenticated node to involve in the communication. The rank is designed with reputation value in the ranking model. The ranking model clusters the nodes efficiently and selects the cluster head for an improved outcome in packet transmission. The cluster head is elected from the group formation based on the best threshold value of nodes. In order to enhance the lifespan of the network, the secret key is created and circulated by all cluster heads.

Authenticated group key agreement protocol chooses the secret key in authenticating group. As a result, not only the malicious nodes are avoided, the node attack and communication failure are also avoided. The authenticated group key agreement protocol also guides to pass the packet data in an efficient manner. The performance evaluation showed that the secure key model supports secure communication in ad hoc network in terms of malicious node detection efficiency, node reputation, performance rate in node clustering and computational cost. The results also showed 30% higher percentage in detecting malicious node, improving the security in MANET. Finally, SKM performs well in providing secure communication over the nodes in the network.

The hybrid approach for node co-operation based clustering in MANET is based on the node cooperativeness range reducing the chance of message loss. After estimating the cooperativeness range of each node, the reorganization of nodes take place in its own. In order to improve the lifespan of the network, node cooperativeness range is computed. Based on the range, the clustering and communication process is done. Then, the clustering of node is carried out efficiently and the CH is elected for enhancing the good transmission over the network. As a result, not only the malevolent nodes are discarded, the communication failures are also highly reduced. Finally, the hybrid approach for node cooperation based clustering enhances the security level through forecasting weightage of node cooperativeness and increases network lifespan by self-organizing the nodes. The experimental results showed that the hybrid approach for node cooperation based clustering perform well in a secure communication over the nodes in the MANET network in terms of node cooperativeness of about 20-25% compared to an existing FESCIM model and ERP-SCDS.

Efficient node cooperation and security mechanism defeats the existence of selfish nodes in MANET with node cooperation by generating authentication among nodes through node cooperation. The ENCS mechanism supports high security by eliminating the misbehavior nodes from replacing the security associations with unidentified nodes. Security associations are only replaced with nodes in trusted community, enhancing the security inside group of trusted nodes. Security associations presented the realization of features in every node inside the group. The security features are selected based on the validation of common usage of nodes in the specified network. Experimental results showed that the ECNS mechanism outperforms well in terms of packet transmission efficiency, average information leakage, average cost and security level in the range of 15-25% high compared to the existing value iteration algorithm and ODMRP-HT.

Routing aware packet reserving framework in MANET considers the end to end routing condition with maximal throughput. RAPR is complimentary system where the packet reserve utilizes local routing information. The local routing holds the information of the node clustering, node co-operation and security level. RAPR follows the approach of shortest path travel earlier approach. The mobile nodes select the packet which travels in shortest distance earlier from the queue to reduce the delay count. Path setup in RAPR estimates the security level of the system, and symbolizes the end-to-end routing by controlling the clogging. RAPR reaches the packet to the destination with high probability ratio and minimal delay count. Simulation results attain the maximal network security level, end to end throughput rate and resource utilization efficiency. On the other hand simulation results also reduce the communication overhead, cost and delay time in RAPR framework. Finally, RAPR designed to perform effective resource utilization with 15.3% improved end to end throughput maintenance.

7.2   FUTURE WORK

The security of the communication is enhanced in the secure key model with the utilization of reputation system, ranking in node clustering and group key agreement protocol. As the ranking process involves calculation of nodes activity and computation of forwarding time, it results in high computational cost. Future work may be planned to reduce the computational time. In group key agreement the fact that a group member will compute a bad key remains unnoticed, mostly if the group is huge. As authenticated group key management prevents any exchange of messages only with two users.

However, there are limitations of reputation based mechanism. First, as there is a probability of collision, a packet obviously drops even in the nonexistence of a selfish node. This makes it hard to determine whether the packet drop is due to normal reasons or selfish behavior of node. Second, the selfish nodes isolated from the network using reputation based scheme cannot be used in data forwarding.

Hybrid approach in node cooperation based clustering will be unable to co-operate nodes, if data is forwarded using a different path without complaint. Another limitation of node cooperation is when a node has enough recognition to send its own data; it decides not to cooperate anymore and starts dropping packets. Further, efficient technique will be required to control the dropping of packets, if node cooperation fails. Again in efficient node cooperation and security mechanism the time taken to evaluate quantitative trust value is high. Future work may plan in reducing the time consumption of evaluating trust values.

REFERENCES

1. Abbas, S, Merabti, M & Llewellyn-Jones, D 2010, 'Deterring Whitewashing Attacks in Reputation Based Schemes for Mobile Ad hoc Network', Proceedings of Wireless Days(WD), Venice, Italy, pp. 1-6.

2. Altman, E & De Pellegrini, F 2011, 'Forward Correction and Fountain Codes in Delay-Tolerant Networks', IEEE/ACM Transactions on Networking, vol. 19, no. 1, pp. 1-13.

3. Altman, E, Basar, T & De Pellegrini, F 2008, 'Optimal Monotone Forwarding Policies in Delay Tolerant Mobile Ad hoc Networks', Proceedings of the 8th International Symposium on Modeling and Optimization in Mobile, Ad Hoc and Wireless Networks, Avignon, France, pp. 497-504.

4. Ashok Kumar, Vinod Kumar & Chand, N 2011, 'Energy Efficient Clustering and Cluster Head Rotation Scheme for Wireless Sensor Networks', International Journal of Advanced Computer Science and Applications, vol. 3, no. 5, pp. 129-136.

5. Bernasconi, R, Giordano, S, Puiatti, A, Bruno, R & Gregori, E 2007, 'Design and Implementation of an Enhanced 802.11 MAC Architecture for Single-Hop Wireless Networks', ACM Transaction on Wireless Communications and Networking, vol. 2007, no. 1, pp. 33-33.

6. Bhatnagar, MR, Hjorungnes, A & Debbah, M 2010, 'Delay-Tolerant Decode-and-Forward Based Cooperative Communication over Ricean Channels', IEEE Transactions on Wireless Communications, vol. 9, no. 4, pp. 1277-1282.

7. Bhorkar, AA, Naghshvar, M, Javidi, T & Rao, BD 2012, 'An Adaptive Opportunistic Routing Scheme for Wireless Ad hoc Networks', IEEE/ACM Transactions on Networking, vol. 20, no. 1, pp. 2838-2842.

8   Bu, S, Yu, FR, Liu, XP & Tang, H 2011, 'Structural Results for Combined Continuous User Authentication and Intrusion Detection in High Security Mobile Ad hoc Networks', IEEE Transactions on Wireless Communications, vol. 10, no. 9, pp. 3064-3073.

9   Choi, JH, Shim, KS, Lee, SK & Wu, KL 2012, 'Handling Selfishness in Replica Allocation over a Mobile Ad Hoc Network', IEEE Transactions on Mobile Computing, vol. 11, no. 2, pp. 278-291.

10 Chuah, M & Yang, P 2009, 'Impact of Selective Dropping Attacks on Network Coding Performance in DTNs and a Potential Mitigation Scheme', Proceedings of the 18th International Conference on Computer Communications and Networks, San Francisco, California, pp. 1-6.

11 Cohen, R & Kapchits, B 2011, 'Continuous Neighbor Discovery in Asynchronous Sensor Networks', IEEE/ACM Transactions on Networking, vol. 19, no. 1, pp. 69-79.

12 Daly, EM & Haahr, M 2009, 'Social Network Analysis for Information Flow in Disconnected Delay-Tolerant MANETs', IEEE Transactions on Mobile Computing, vol. 8, no. 5, pp. 606-621.

13 Dang, H & Wu, H 2010, 'Clustering and Cluster-Based Routing Protocol for Delay-Tolerant Mobile Networks', IEEE Transactions on Wireless Communications, vol. 9, no. 6, pp. 1874-1881.

14 Dini, G & Duca, AL 2012, 'Towards a reputation-based routing protocol to contrast blackholes in a delay tolerant network', Journal of Ad hoc Networks, vol. 10, no. 7, pp. 1167-1178.

15 Dong, J, Curtmola, R & Nita-Rotaru, C 2011, 'Secure High-Throughput Multicast Routing in Wireless Mesh Networks', IEEE Transactions on Mobile Computing, vol. 10, no. 5, pp. 653-668.

16 Fadlullah, ZM, Taleb, T, Vasilakos, AV, Guizani, M & Kato, N 2010, 'DTRAB: Combating Against Attacks on Encrypted Protocols through Traffic-Feature Analysis', IEEE/ACM Transactions on Networking, vol. 18, no. 4, pp. 1234-1247.

17 Fan, Y, Jiang, Y, Zhuv, H, Chen, J & Shen, X 2011, 'Network Coding Based Privacy Preservation against Traffic Analysis in Multi-Hop Wireless Networks', IEEE Transactions on Wireless Communications, vol. 10, no. 3, pp. 834-843.

18   Feng, KT, Lin, JS & Lei, WN 2013, 'Design and Analysis of Adaptive Receiver Transmission Protocols for Receiver Blocking Problem in Wireless Ad hoc Networks', IEEE Transactions on Mobile Computing, vol. 12, no. 8, pp. 1651-1668.

19   Guan, Q, Yu, FR, Jiang, S & Leung, VCM 2012, 'Joint Topology Control and Authentication Design in Mobile Ad Hoc Networks With Cooperative Communications', IEEE Transactions on Vehicular Technology, vol. 61, no. 6, pp. 2674-2685.

20   Han, S, Tian, B, He, M & Chang, E 2009, 'Efficient Threshold Self-Healing Key Distribution with Sponsorization for Infrastructureless Wireless Networks', IEEE Transactions on Wireless Communications, vol. 8, no. 4, pp. 1876-1887.

21   Hara, T 2010, 'Quantifying Impact of Mobility on Data Availability in Mobile Ad Hoc Networks', IEEE Transactions on Mobile Computing, vol. 9, no. 2, pp. 241-258.

22   He, D, Bu, J, Chan, S, Chen, C & Yin, M 2011, 'Privacy Preserving Universal Authentication Protocol for Wireless Communications', IEEE Transactions on Wireless Communications, vol. 10, no. 2, pp. 431-436.

23   Ji, Z, Yu, W & Liu, KJR 2006, 'Cooperation Enforcement in Autonomous MANETs under Noise and Imperfect Observation', Proceedings of the 3rd Annual IEEE Communication Society on Sensor and Ad Hoc Communications and Networks, vol. 2, Reston, Virginia, pp. 460-468.

24   Ji, Z, Yu, W & Liu, KJR 2006 'Belief-Based Packet Forwarding in Self-Organized Mobile Ad Hoc Networks with Noise and Imperfect Observation', Proceedings of the Conference on Wireless Communications and Networking, Las Vegas, Nevada, United States, vol. 1, pp. 343-348.

25   Jiang, C, Shi, Y, Hou, YT & Kompella, S 2011, 'On the Asymptotic Capacity of Multi-Hop MIMO Ad Hoc Networks', IEEE Transactions on Wireless Communications, vol. 10, no. 4, pp. 1032-1037.

26   Khokhar, RH, & Ngadi, M & Mandala, S 2010, 'A Review of Current Routing Attacks in Mobile Ad Hoc Networks', International Journal of Computer Science and Security, vol. 2, no. 3, pp. 18-29.

27	Krifa, A, Barakat, C & Spyropoulos, T 2008, 'Optimal Buffer Management Policies for Delay Tolerant Networks', Proceedings of the 5th Annual IEEE Communication Society Conference on Sensor, Mesh and Ad Hoc Communications and Networks, San Francisco, California, pp. 260-268.

28	Kumar, A, Kadam, V, Kumar, S & Pawar, S 2011, 'An Acknowledgement-Based Approach for the Detection of Routing Misbehavior in MANETS', International Journal of Advances in Embedded Systems, vol. 1, no. 1, pp. 4-6.

29	Kun, M & Li, L 2014, 'An Efficient Pairwise Key Predistribution Scheme for Wireless Sensor Networks', Journal of Networks, vol. 9, no. 2, pp. 277-282.

30	Kwon, T, Lee, JH & Song, JS 2009, 'Location-Based Pairwise Key Predistribution for Wireless Sensor Networks', IEEE Transactions on Wireless Communications, vol. 8, no. 11, pp. 5436-5442.

31	Li, LC & Liu, RS 2010, 'Securing Cluster-Based Ad Hoc Networks with Distributed Authorities', IEEE Transactions on Wireless Communications, vol. 9, no. 10, pp. 3072-3081.

32	Liu, K, Deng, J, Varshneey, PK & Balakrishnan, K 2007, 'An Acknowledgement Based Approach for the Detection of Routing Misbehaviour in MANETs', IEEE Transactions on Mobile Computing, vol. 6, no. 5, pp. 536-550.

33	Llewellyn, LC, Hopkinson, KM & Graham, SR 2011, 'Distributed Fault-Tolerant Quality of Wireless Networks', IEEE Transactions on Mobile Computing, vol. 10, no. 2, pp. 175-190.

34	Mamatha, GS & Sharma, SC 2010, 'A Highly Secured Approach against Attacks in MANETS', International Journal of Computer Theory and Engineering, vol. 2, no. 5, pp. 815-819.

35	Mani, P & Kamalakkannan, P 2013, 'Mitigating Selfish Behavior in Mobile Ad Hoc Networks: A Survey', International Journal of Computer Applications, vol. 73, no.22, pp. 1-7.

36	Mohmoud, MMEA & Shen, X 2012, 'FESCIM: Fair, Efficient, and Secure Cooperation Incentive Mechanism for Multi-hop Cellular Networks', IEEE Transaction on Mobile Computing, vol. 11, no. 5, pp. 753-766.

37 Nishiyama, H, Ngo, T, Ansari, N & Kato, N 2012, 'On Minimizing the Impact of Mobility on Topology Control in Mobile Ad Hoc Networks', IEEE Transactions on Wireless Communications, vol. 11, no. 3, pp. 1158-1166.

38 Ozdemir, S & Çam, H 2010, 'Integration of False Data Detection with Data Aggregation and Confidential Transmission in Wireless Sensor Networks', IEEE/ACM Transactions on Networking, vol. 18, no. 3, pp. 736-749.

39 Pankaj Kumar Sehgal & Rajender Nath 2009, 'An Encryption Based Dynamic and Secure Routing Protocol for Mobile Ad Hoc Network', International Journal of Computer Science and Security, vol. 3, no. 1, pp. 16-22.

40 Praveen Sam, R, Chandrasekhar Reddy, P & Stephen Charles, B 2008, 'Dual factor routing protocol for mobile ad hoc networks', African Journal of Mathematics and Computer Science Research, vol. 1, no. 1, pp. 10-19.

41 Rossi, M, Tapparello, C & Tomasin, S 2011, 'On Optimal Cooperator Selection Policies for Multi-Hop Ad Hoc Networks', IEEE Transactions on Wireless Communications, vol. 10, no. 2, pp. 506-518.

42 Sadek, AK, Su, W & Liu, KJR 2007, 'Multinode Cooperative Communications in Wireless Networks', IEEE Transactions on Signal Processing, vol. 55, no. 1, pp. 341-355.

43 Sankara Gomathi, S & Bhagyaveni, MA 2008, 'Secured On Demand Position Based Private Routing Protocol for mobile ad hoc network (SO2P)', Journal of Computer Science, Informatics and Electrical Engineering, vol. 2, no. 1, pp. 1-12.

44 Shu, T & Krunz, M 2010, 'Coverage-Time Optimization for Clustered Wireless Sensor Networks: A Power-Balancing Approach', IEEE/ACM Transactions on Networking, vol. 18, no. 1, pp. 202-215.

45 Shu, T, Krunz, M & Liu, S 2010, 'Secure Data Collection in Wireless Sensor Networks Using Randomized Dispersive Routes', IEEE Transactions on Mobile Computing, vol. 9, no. 7, pp. 941-954.

46 Shoba, L & Neha, B 2014, 'Handling Node Self-Centeredness in replica allocation Over MANET', International Journal of Emerging Trends & Technology in Computer Science, vol. 3, no. 2, pp. 121-122.

47   Su, MY 2011, 'Prevention of selective blackhole attacks on mobile ad hoc networks through intrusion detection system', Journal of Computer Communications, vol. 34, no. 1, pp. 107-117.

48   Sumathy, S & Upendra Kumar, B 2010, 'Secure key exchange and encryption mechanism for group communication in wireless ad hoc networks', Journal of Graph Theory in Wireless Ad hoc Networks and Sensor Networks, vol. 12, no. 1, pp. 9-16.

49   Wan, Z, Ren, K & Gu, M 2012, 'USOR: An Unobservable Secure On-Demand Routing Protocol for Mobile Ad Hoc Networks', IEEE Transactions on Wireless Communications, vol. 11, no. 5, pp. 1922-1932.

50   Yang, S, Yeo, CK & Lee, BS 2012, 'Toward Reliable Data Delivery for Highly Dynamic Mobile Ad Hoc Networks', IEEE Transactions on Mobile Computing, vol. 11, no. 1, pp. 111-124.

51   Yogita, W, Vidya, D & Pankaj, V 2014, 'Key Management with Improved Location Aided Cluster Based Routing Protocol in MANETs', Proceedings of the 3rd International Conference on Frontiers of Intelligent Computing: Theory and Applications (FICTA), vol. 2, pp. 687-695.

52   Yu, J, Qi, Y, Wang, G & Gu, X 2012, 'A cluster-based routing protocol for wireless sensor networks with nonuniform node distribution', International Journal of Electronics and Communications, vol. 66, no. 1, pp. 54-61.

53   Yuen, WH, Mau, SC & Yates, RD 2009, 'Existence of Data and Multiuser Diversities in Noncooperative Mobile Infostation Networks', IEEE Transactions on Mobile Computing, vol. 8, no. 8, pp. 1117-1131.

54   Zhang, C, Song, Y, Fang, Y & Zhang, Y 2011, 'On the Price of Security in Large-Scale Wireless Ad Hoc Networks', IEEE/ACM Transactions on Networking, vol. 19, no. 2, pp. 319-332.

55   Zhou, X, Ganti, RK & Andrews, JG 2011, 'Secure Wireless Network Connectivity with Multi-Antenna Transmission', IEEE Transactions on Wireless Communications, vol. 10, no. 2, pp. 425-430.